Martial Arts
of the Mind
for Teachers

An Arsenal of Powerful Approaches to
Combat Teachers' Daily Challenges

Paul T.Morelli

the Peppertree Press
Sarasota, Florida

Copyright ©Paul T. Morelli, 2010

All rights reserved. Published by the Peppertree Press, LLC. the Peppertree Press and associated logos are trademarks of the Peppertree Press, LLC.

For information regarding permission,
call 941-922-2662 or contact us at our website:
www.peppertreepublishing.com or write to:
the Peppertree Press, LLC.
Attention: Publisher
1269 First Street, Suite 7
Sarasota, Florida 34236

ISBN: 978-1-936343-06-5

Library of Congress Number: 2010928150

Printed in the U.S.A.

Printed June 2010

This book is dedicated to the excellent teachers who are no longer with us. Their contributions made a difference in the lives of so many.

MARTIAL ARTS OF THE MIND FOR TEACHERS

TABLE OF CONTENTS

TABLE OF CONTENTS (CONT.)

Acknowledgments

Many thanks go to my family, friends and all individuals who influenced me in developing this book.

To Cynthia Kilgallon and Jan White, who first suggested and encouraged me to write this book, I thank you.

Thanks to Bill Rauhauser for his instruction, suggestions and help, especially in the "Just a Thought" sections.

Special thanks go to the teachers and staff at Carroll Hill Elementary School, who were both excellent teachers and great energizer buddies.

To the teachers, administrators, staff, students and parents with whom I had the privilege to connect and learn, thanks so much.

To all of the senseis, sempais and sifus who instructed me, a respectful thank you. Special thanks goes to sensei: George, Bonnie, Irv, Duwayne (Pee Wee), Darrell, and sifu Rich.

An utmost respectful thank you goes to Shihan Mitsugi Saotome and Shihan Hiroshi Ikeda for their leadership in the Aikido Schools of Ueshiba organization. Also, for their mastery in the skills of aikido that perpetuates this martial art to be a lifelong journey.

Thanks to all of my training partners in the Albany Aikido Dojo and the ASU of Sarasota Dojo. I also want to thank the people that I trained with many years ago in the karate dojo and kung fu school.

To my daughter, Aimee, and my son, Jeffrey, for their creative work on the cover of this book and for their support in this endeavor, I thank you.

Thank you to my daughter, Kari, for her ongoing interest, support and encouragement throughout the writing process.

Thanks to my parents Tim and Doris, for their guidance in stressing the importance of a college education.

Heartfelt and special thanks go to my loving wife, Rose Ann, for the many hours that she gave in discussing, proofreading, suggesting, supporting and encouraging me throughout this entire process. She is both the love of my life and my hero.

Lastly, thanks to Almighty God for the gifts that made this possible.

Chapter 1

By George, "I Think You've Got It"

"A mighty flame followeth a tiny spark."
Dante

The Birth and Evolution of
Martial Arts of the Mind for Teachers

THE BEGINNING

My first college class in education would ignite a spark that would produce a lasting flame in my career as a teacher. The professor started this class by posing the following question, "Twenty years from now, will you be a teacher who has twenty years of experience, or a teacher who taught one year twenty times?"

This question would prove to be a very powerful force that would guide me throughout my professional life. It brought me to the realization that I wanted to be a teacher, who would learn, improve and progress every year; anything shy of this would be unacceptable.

This focus, along with an innate hunger to perform at a very high level, stayed with me throughout my 32 years in education. Learning became a lifetime pursuit.

THE POWER OF A CUP OF COFFEE

During the time I was taking this education class, I would soon discover that having a simple cup of coffee in the student center could prove to be an equally important event. On a Monday morning at 7:30, I was having a cup of coffee with my friend, George, who was a student in my study group. We were discussing an assignment for the upcoming class. A student named Mike, who was sitting at a table behind us, grabbed George from behind and attempted to put him in a choke hold. Coffee and coffee cups went flying everywhere. Now, George had Mike in a choke hold. While in this painful and compromising position, Mike apologized and claimed that he was just fooling around. It was quite obvious that he was trying to show off to his friends. George, slowly and gently released Mike. There was complete silence in that area of the student center for the next few moments. Without saying anything, everyone got up and headed to their 8:00 class.

While having lunch with George later that day, we discussed the unfortunate incident that occurred in the student center. Upon questioning him about his instant response to Mike's aggression, he credited it to the training he had in both the armed forces and in karate. Although I thought that the speed and power of his technique was extraordinary, George claimed that it was merely a standard self-defense technique. He didn't think it was such a big deal.

However, there was something other than George's speed and technique that was even more impressive—it was George's attitude and disposition. He stayed cool, calm, and was under control during this entire episode. George didn't make a big deal of it. Instead he got an unsuspecting attacker under control and then showed his attacker compassion by releasing him. I believe George was able to do this, because he didn't seem to possess fear. At no time did George grandstand or brag—instead, he had a humble attitude. That really impressed the heck out of me.

THE BIRTH OF MARTIAL ARTS OF THE MIND FOR TEACHERS

The more that I reflected on the incident in the student center, the more it seemed profound. It was obvious to me that George was a very confident individual who possessed superior physical skills. His focus was like a powerful laser beam and nothing seemed to alter, distract, or impede it.

He also displayed some exemplary character traits, such as humility, fearlessness, compassion and kindness. All these skills and traits were demonstrated instantaneously in the face of adversity. George had the total package of physical skills along with some very impressive character traits.

This response was something some people may preach about, but it was the first time that I witnessed such an extraordinary event. Instantly, I experienced a deep desire to possess all these traits and skills. This was what I needed to enable me become a better teacher.

As teachers, it is our responsibility to stay calm, cool and collected. Quality teachers try never to intentionally lose their temper. The incident in the student center, along with the discussion in my education class, gave birth to my first thoughts of *Martial Arts of the Mind for Teachers*.

A few days after the incident, a group of us approached George to see if he was interested in teaching us karate. He agreed to teach us. However, we had to agree to several conditions. First, we had to always be on time for class. Second, we would have to be serious and hard-working students. Lastly, he would not take any money to teach us, because he strongly believed that teaching karate was a privilege and an honor.

We trained very hard with George for two years. He helped us strengthen our bodies, techniques, minds, character and spirit. Just before we graduated from college and during our last karate training session, George evaluated us. He individually told us our strengths and weaknesses.

The source of the title to this chapter was taken from George's evaluation of me. He believed that I acquired the necessary skills to be a very effective martial artist. After graduating from college, we went our separate ways. Graduation marked the end of instruction from George, and the beginning of a lifelong connection of martial arts with education.

THE EVOLUTION OF MARTIAL ARTS OF THE MIND FOR TEACHERS

After college, I held the following positions in an urban public school system, which enveloped my next 32 years in education:

- High School Teacher
- High School Assistant Principal
- Elementary Principal

OTHER TEACHING EXPERIENCES:

- Volunteer Teacher, Elementary Level
- Adjunct Teacher, Community College
- Adjunct Teacher, 4-Year College -Developed Leadership Institute
- Gave seminars to school administrators on leadership

VALUABLE SIGNIFICANT EXPERIENCES:

- Trained in the Martial Arts of Karate, Kung Fu and Aikido
- Studied in the field of self improvement

These experiences produced an intrapersonal synergy that developed and fine-tuned a repertoire of teacher weapons, which have been paramount to my success and enjoyment in the teaching profession.

I used these powerful weapons over and over in dealing with the many challenges that I encountered each day in school. It took more than 30 years to progress to the point of writing this book.

The next 13 chapters will arm teachers with powerful weapons to help them with their teaching challenges. These weapons **are allowed** in school. So let's get started.

Just a Thought ...

The road to success is always under construction.

 Chapter 2

A Powerful Focus: Do You Have Eyes in the Back of Your Head?

"The superior fighter succeeds without violence. The greatest conqueror wins without a struggle . . ."

Lao Tsu, Tao Teb King

A Powerful Focus

A MARTIAL ARTS FOCUS

Conscientious martial artists are continually striving to bring their focus to a higher level. Achieving an exemplary focus helps improve an overall skill level. Teachers must continually work at five areas in pursuing a powerful focus: peripheral vision, sharper hearing, anticipation with good timing, proper posture, and a controlled breathing pattern. These areas will enable you to achieve a powerful focus as a martial artist and teacher. So can you have eyes in the back of your head?

A TEACHER'S POWERFUL FOCUS

We all possess the ability to focus. Bringing it up to a new level is what's needed. One of the most powerful tools a martial artist can possess is developing the ability to focus intensely. If you train and increase your abilities in this area, it can help you to become a better teacher. It can also enable you to perform your job with passion, and at the same time, be serene and patient.

How? You can expand the awareness of what is going on in your classroom. The students' receptiveness to presentations will become instantly clear. When making presentations, teacher adaptability will flow harmoniously. However, the greatest benefit is the ability to attain an intense level of concentration on demand. In other words, it is like being in "The zone." This is the ability to block out the superficial and have a laser-beam type focus on the important areas. It can greatly improve your effectiveness, both personally and professionally.

Once you've given your attention to focusing, it won't take long before the benefits will be apparent. So what is involved in helping to improve the power of one's focus? Practicing and applying daily the concepts of expanded peripheral vision, sharper hearing, anticipation and good timing will enable you to achieve a powerful focus.

After a while, this skill will become part of your behavior and add to your arsenal of teacher weapons. You may be surprised at how quickly this can be achieved. So let's get to the first area of focus, which is peripheral vision.

Expanded Peripheral Vision

Training in martial arts helped me come to the realization that I was neglecting the use of my peripheral vision. I would constantly turn my head to see what was going on. I needed to increase my range of peripheral vision in the classroom throughout the day. This enabled me to clearly see the students who were off task, and immediately direct them back to the task at hand.

SHARPER HEARING

In martial arts, we were trained to connect our abilities to focus, see and hear. There were training sessions in the *dojo* (martial arts school) at night when the lights were turned off. This forced us to rely on our hearing. We couldn't see our attackers until it was too late. We had to use sharper hearing, while executing the appropriate techniques.

Our skills improved over time. So an application was made in these hearing skills to the classroom. Using an expanded peripheral vision, along with sharper hearing, can significantly improve your focus.

However, your students may not be thrilled about these newly discovered skills. This experience was especially true for me, for instance, when I caught students engaging in gossip. Their response was, "How can he possibly hear what we're saying?" These simple skills have been a great help to me over the years. Anyone can develop and use these skills, and you don't have to be a martial artist to reap their benefits. All it takes is daily practice.

There are other instances when these skills could be very helpful in the classroom. For example, when giving a student some individual help during class, use your peripheral vision and keen hearing on the rest of the class. This will enable you to keep the other students on task.

Also, when writing on the board or using a computer, rely on these skills and the students might comment, "How can he/she do two things at once?" What a benefit it is for a teacher not to constantly direct students to stay on task. Keep practicing these skills, and they will eventually become second nature.

ANTICIPATION AND GOOD TIMING

Anticipation and good timing are very important skills to have when practicing martial arts. You can have excellent form and technique, but without anticipation, a technique by itself is useless. If your timing is off or disrupted, the technique will also be ineffective. With the proper anticipation and good timing, positive momentum develops and execution of the technique is easy.

This is also true for teachers. Teachers spend a great deal of time developing lesson plans. In these plans, the teacher decides what techniques, strategies, materials, and methodologies are chosen in anticipation of students' needs. Good timing in the execution of the lesson is connected to the sequence that we chose in our lesson plan.

There are many instances when teachers have to deviate and change their lesson plans. This adjustment may require re-establishing a positive momentum. These same concepts of good timing with anticipation could be used helping teachers with their students to develop a more intense focus and concentration.

Teachers have been told never to have their backs face the class. This is not always possible. It's especially true when working at the chalkboard, whiteboard or simply helping a student individually. Anticipation and good timing are great to use in these circumstances.

Teachers may know in advance when students may try certain things. Using peripheral vision, sharpened hearing and anticipation with good timing can make it very easy for teachers to correct students, while working at the board. This may even get some students to think you have eyes in the back of your head.

PROPER POSTURE

Proper posture is another element in enhancing our focusing skills. In martial arts, we constantly strive to have proper posture. This brings with it many benefits, such as balance, advantageous angles, readiness and a feeling of confidence. The appearance of proper posture has a powerful effect on how others perceive and react to you. This is reinforced by looking at a trained soldier's posture, and the positive message that it sends. So how can we get proper posture?

Proper posture can be attained with a minimal amount of effort. It should be noted, that you are not striving to look like a soldier going to the battlefield. Instead, you want to be seen as a positive, relaxed, and confident person.

For instance, I found that dropping my chin can produce negative feelings, while having my chin up promotes a positive feeling. If I am in a state of sadness, it takes more effort for me to keep my chin up. This not only works for me, but has helped many students and colleagues.

Proper posture requires us to have our feet shoulder-width apart. Shoulders should always be down, and relaxed. This importance is reinforced in martial arts. When an attacker's shoulders are up, we are taught they are out of balance and in a weakened position. The spine should be straight and the position of the chin should be parallel to the floor. Heads should be up and eyes should be facing straight ahead. Proper posture is an added feature to enhancing our focusing skills. Don't underestimate the power of having proper posture. It truly can make a big difference.

CONTROLLED BREATHING PATTERN

Breathing is the final but most important element in bringing the power of focus to a higher level. In martial arts, proper breathing is so critical; it is included in the instruction of every technique. The benefits in attending to our breathing pattern are enormous. Before taking martial arts, I only paid attention to my breathing when I was out of breath while participating in sports.

Breathing should be natural and not forced. When labored breathing due to stress or exercise is reached, this should trigger an adjustment to our breathing. The point of hyperventilating or going into panic mode needs to be averted.

Practice the following breathing techniques that are taught in martial arts. Inhale by taking air in through the nose, letting it settle in the lower belly (*hara* in Japanese) momentarily, and then exhale slowly through the mouth. The sound of breathing should not be excessively loud.

Practice this technique daily. When attending meetings that are truly frustrating and challenging, practice controlled breathing and you will be able to stay in a healthy state of mind. You may also need to use this method when controlling misbehaviors in the classroom or when attending a conference with an especially difficult parent.

Proper breathing enables you to be cool, calm, and under control with a great deal more patience. Controlling your breathing enables you to control your thinking. If you don't correct short and shallow breathing, your emotions will control you.

A teacher's controlled breathing pattern can help transform a seemingly unsuccessful parent conference into a successful one. Keep in mind, it is not how a difficult parent starts a conference that is most important—rather, it is their state of mind at the end of the conference.

Please consider putting into practice these suggestions. They are pragmatic teacher weapons that can be used every single day, in and out of the classroom. You can work on them one at a time or all together. So take your time and think of the positive and powerful effects these weapons can have on you as a teacher.

Well, do you have eyes in the back of your head? Only your students can answer that question.

END OF CHAPTER TEACHER WEAPONS REVIEW

From this point forward, at the end each chapter; there will be a capsulated review of the teacher weapons. This section summarizes the weapons that are contained in each chapter. It should provide you with a quick reference that will assist you without having to re-read the entire chapter. So get going and start to use your martial arts of the mind weapons and begin to feel the power.

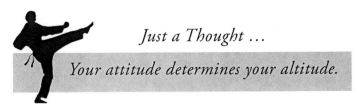

Just a Thought ...

Your attitude determines your altitude.

Chapter 2: Teacher Weapons Review

WEAPON: DEVELOP A POWERFUL FOCUS

1. Practice and use expanded peripheral vision throughout the day
2. Practice and develop sharper hearing, instead of relying on vision alone
3. Utilize anticipation with good timing
4. Practice proper posture daily:
   > Chin up
   > Spine straight
   > Shoulders down & relaxed
   > Eyes forward
5. Be aware of your breathing pattern:
   Note: This pattern should not be outwardly noticeable
   > Intake air through nose
   > Have air settle in lower abdomen
   > Exhale slowly through your mouth

Practice these weapons every day. In a week's time, you will see noticeable improvements. With each passing week, the amount of focus and concentration should increase, while the amount of effort decreases.

In about two months, it should become second nature, and don't be surprised if the results are incredible. So don't delay, start using these weapons and experience the power they can bring to you and your classroom.

Chapter 3

Are You a Pointer or a Retriever?

"The noble man seeks what he wants in himself;
the inferior man seeks it from others."

Confucius
(The Analects)

Pointer or Retriever

POINTER

Pointers do a whole lot of negative talking and very little work to make things better. They don't hesitate to point out other people's faults, while they ignore their own idiosyncrasies. Gossip is not beneath them. They become very good in the art of complaining.

Pointers often use excuses and may blame others, while taking very little responsibility. They expect others to fix things for them, because they get stuck on the problem and contribute very little toward the solution. Pointers have a negative impact on themselves, their audience, and their school.

RETRIEVER

Retrievers are hard working, consummate professionals. They are enthusiastic and work well under all types of conditions. They are doers and spend a great deal of time working on (retrieving) the solution. Retrievers are fun to be around and project a positive image.

There are, however, some teachers who may begin to spend too much time in the teacher's lounge. These teachers are referred to as "Lounge Lizards." While they are otherwise great teachers, they can get caught up in negative discussions or "Coffee Pot Seminars." This behavior can transform positive outlooks into negative ones, changing retrievers into pointers.

I must admit there have been times when the "pointer" in me would rear its ugly head. However, by using the weapons in this chapter, I was able to get back into "retriever" mode.

MARTIAL ARTS OF THE MIND WEAPONS FOR TEACHERS

Being a high school teacher during the day and a student of martial arts at night, there were mornings when it was very difficult to get ready for work. The aches and pains placed me in slow motion. I had thoughts like, "Why am I doing this?" "It's too hard." "I just don't need this right now in my life." "I have enough to do with the demands of my job and family."

Then it hit me—making excuses was just what some of my students were doing to escape their responsibilities, especially homework assignments. I was taking the same path. Some excuses they used were the standard, run-of-the-mill ones like, "This homework is too hard," or "I really did my homework last night, but I forgot it on the kitchen table," and let's not forget the ever popular, "The dog ate my homework."

Once in a while, someone came up with a really creative excuse, such as, "I was in a car accident last night after I did your assignment, and the car caught on fire and destroyed everything, including my car." Well, that was a good one! The student was "busted", since he came to class with his textbook that was supposedly destroyed.

I'm sure you've heard your share of excuses. Some of them might be better than others, while others are outright ridiculous. The fact is excuses enable us to take the easy way out.

I was now determined to continue in martial arts. This determined attitude is what we expect from the students and is also expected of teachers. From this point on, this experience enabled me to develop an honorable martial arts attitude.

An Honorable Martial Arts Attitude

In the *dojo*, (Japanese for the place of martial arts training), a student's attitude is extremely important. It is unacceptable to make excuses or have an attitude that is negative, lazy or passive. Students who are giving a half-hearted effort in the *dojo* are asked to sit out. All students are expected to give it their all throughout the entire session.

If we are doing our very best and things still don't go the way we want them to in the *dojo*, the only recourse is to continue to work hard and keep a determined attitude. There is no placing blame on others. You must, instead, look within you.

Complaining is dishonorable and out of the question. If one is truly tired, the option is to sit or kneel properly out of the way. Making fun of others is not tolerated; in a *dojo*, it can actually be hazardous to one's health. Doing 30 pushups on your knuckles on a hardwood floor allows one to learn this lesson very quickly. Correction is only to be given by the *sensei* (teacher) or a *sempai* (senior student).

Lastly, it is every person's responsibility in the *dojo* to generate a positive energy that contributes in fostering an atmosphere of harmony and respect. This is all possible, if one keeps an honorable martial arts attitude. Can you imagine what the benefits would be if an honorable attitude was the norm in the classroom?

AN HONORABLE ATTITUDE IN THE CLASSROOM

If a teacher and his students strive to have an honorable attitude in the classroom, it can result in exemplary teacher and student performance. The benefits are nothing short of phenomenal. These outstanding performances authenticated that an honorable attitude in the classroom is an excellent martial arts of the mind weapon. While the benefits of an honorable attitude in the classroom are easy to see, the challenge is putting them into practice.

How can an honorable martial arts attitude be transferred into your classroom? First, it is the responsibility of both teacher **and** students to generate positive energy that fosters an atmosphere of harmony and respect. This is accomplished by adhering to a list of rules and procedures. This list has been developed from the normal procedures followed in the *dojo* and should be prominently displayed in the classroom:

- We will teach and learn with a determined attitude and a hard work ethic
- We will never have a "give up" attitude
- We will be responsible for our thoughts, words and actions
- We will not place blame on others or make excuses for our actions
- We will not make fun of or tease others
- We will strive to foster harmony and respect in the classroom

At the end of each day, take a moment to evaluate your classroom's progress. Some of the students will accept these rules immediately, while with others it may take longer. Both the teachers and the students need to view their classrooms as an honorable and well-respected place. How each person speaks and acts determines the success of this weapon.

A bit of caution: as a teacher, you will need to be a top performer each day, regardless of the circumstances. This is the same expectation you have of your students. Every day, each person needs to review and evaluate everyone's speech and actions.

After using this weapon, the classroom is transformed to a people-centered atmosphere. A progression is made from accepting mediocre attitudes, to striving for honorable ones. Success in forming a harmonious atmosphere is very possible, and improving the students' academic performance is well within reach.

LEADERSHIP APPLICATION OF AN HONORABLE ATTITUDE IN YOUR SCHOOL

The principal is the positional leader of a school. This type of leader is simply one who was appointed to that specific job. It should not be perceived that the principal is the *only* person who should work and be responsible for making a school the very best. Instead, it is every person's responsibility in that school to promote an atmosphere of harmony and respect. This is *real* leadership.

If this is the expectation in a *dojo*, why don't we have the same expectation in our schools? Can you imagine the benefits of having a school that sets the standard for **everyone** to have an honorable attitude?

The answer is simple. You can, if you use these weapons. The students' behavior and academic performance would improve significantly. The school would change from being teacher or student-centered, to becoming people-centered.

So how can this happen in your school? First, one must realize that in times of trouble, people who rely heavily on positional power try to pull rank on others. On the other hand, real leaders use personal power and collaboration.

Next, **you** must be the one who takes the first step, beginning in your own classroom. Talk about it with other staff members and friends in your school who generally have similar educational ideas. This will start a nucleus of interested teachers.

Once others start to see the benefits that could be had, it will start to interest more people. Just like some of your students will gravitate towards an honorable classroom attitude sooner than others, the same is true of your colleagues. These people are referred to as *early adapters*.

Another bit of caution: there may be some staff members who may not want to have anything to do with it, because they do not want to change their expectations of themselves. They may want to take the easy way out. Don't let this stop you. The benefits and rewards are well worth it.

I worked very hard at having an honorable attitude in the classroom and had the supreme honor of working in a school where eventually 98% of the teachers achieved this attitude. The benefits and rewards were tremendous. When the majority of the teachers are working together, it is referred to as *critical mass*. Don't delay in the leadership application of this powerful weapon. It may take some time to establish a critical mass, but it will be well worth it.

ARRIVING AT THE 90 % SOLUTION

Determination and hard work is at the core of an honorable attitude. Metaphorically, I observed a similar attitude with a specific breed of dog, the Labrador retriever. This dog is bred to retrieve, and nothing seems to prevent it from doing just that. It will jump and swim in a lake or pond in order to retrieve. It doesn't matter what time of the year it is or how cold the water is. This is a very energetic, hard-working and enthusiastic dog.

Like the Labrador retriever, who overcomes challenges that enter in its path, we, in the classroom, continuously strive to learn, regardless of the difficulties. This metaphor led to the development the 90% solution. This means that 10% of your time and energy should be spent on defining a particular problem in measurable terms, while 90% should be spent on retrieving solutions.

Defining the problem in measurable terms allows us to test the effectiveness of the possible solutions we retrieve. Once a problem is defined, there is no more shifting back to the problem.

As a teacher, I arrived at the 90% solution because this is the starting range for the letter grade "A," which is used as a standard of excellence. This weapon was successfully used many times throughout my career. It enables one to shift focus on the solution, rather than being paralyzed by the problem. This paralysis often turns problem-solving meetings into complaining sessions.

Acting as "pointers," people find fault and blame others. Instead of feeling empowered, arguing and frustration results. There is a need to stop "pointing" and start "retrieving."

This transition enables one to arrive at high-quality solutions in a very short period of time. There will be disagreements, but this process will enable you to work smarter. The 90% solution should be utilized whenever problems are encountered, whether working alone or with others. This weapon can be used in almost any situation.

CLASSROOM APPLICATION

There was a student in a college leadership class, who constantly complained about *everything* that was going on in her life. She complained about many things, including her mother, siblings, homework assignments, and clothes.

I tried to help this student, along with all her weary listeners. She was asked, "Do you think you complain often?"

Everyone laughed, including the student. She agreed and stated that even *she* was tired of hearing herself complain.

I asked her to see me after class for some suggestions. Other students also stayed after class because they were interested in hearing the suggestions. This now became a class project.

Students were told that the reason people complain is because they are fixated on the problem and don't shift their time and energy to the solution. By not shifting to the solution, they expect other people to solve their problems. We all agreed that if we wait for other people to solve our problems, it may never happen. A further explanation of the 90% solution was made.

Lastly, they were encouraged to use this weapon each time a complaint was made. This particular class was on a Friday. When the student came back to school on Monday, she looked proud and happy. She couldn't wait to report that the 90% solution immediately helped her and was a life-changing event.

The students who were with her over the weekend confirmed this statement. She thanked me, and said that her parents also thanked me. Her weary classmates also thanked me. Within a three-week period, she no longer felt a need to complain. This student didn't complain after that initial Friday class. In fact, on several occasions, I heard her remind other students to use the 90% solution!

Teachers should not hesitate to use this weapon to solve a problem. It doesn't matter if it is a problem that you are working on alone or with your colleagues. Its power is awesome. So ask yourself this question, "Am I acting like a *pointer* or a *retriever?*" If the answer is "pointer", it's time to use this weapon.

LEADERSHIP APPLICATION OF THE 90% SOLUTION

When there is a need to solve a difficult problem, collaboration is often used. Although it is not an easy approach, it can be a very powerful one. The 90% solution is a teacher weapon that can make collaboration much easier.

It does this by shifting a group of collaborators away from the problem, where a great deal of blaming and pointing occurs. By shifting to the solution at the proper time, collaboration becomes much easier.

We all have the capacity to become real leaders. I urge you to help your principal, colleagues, students, staff and school. Show, through your actions, that the leadership application of the 90% solution is a very useful and powerful one.

In conclusion, I must admit that I am a lover of all dogs. However, I am partial to one breed; you guessed it, the Labrador retriever. I want to give recognition to my black lab, Sheena, for having been a wonderful resource and an even better family member.

Just a Thought ...

Success comes in can's not in cannot's, so focus on the solution—not the problem.

Chapter 3 - Teacher Weapons Review

WEAPON: DEVELOP AN HONORABLE ATTITUDE IN YOUR CLASSROOM

- Teach and learn every day with a determined attitude and a hard-work ethic
- Never have a "give up" attitude
- Be responsible for your thoughts, words and actions
- Do not place blame on others or make excuses for your actions
- Do not make fun or tease others
- Strive to foster harmony and respect in the classroom

WEAPON: USE THE LEADERSHIP APPLICATION OF AN HONORABLE ATTITUDE IN YOUR SCHOOL

- You must be the one who takes the first step; begin in your own classroom
- Talk about it with other staff members in your school
- Once others start to see the benefits, they will become interested
- Your school will become people-centered

WEAPON: THE 90% SOLUTION

- 90% of your time and energy is spent on the solutions to the problems
- 10% of your time and energy is spent on defining the problems in measurable terms
- Once a problem is defined, shift to the solution—don't shift back to the problem

- Be solutions-oriented instead of problems-focused
- Pointers get paralyzed by the problem
- Retrievers shift from defining the problem to working on the solution

WEAPON: LEADERSHIP APPLICATION OF THE 90% SOLUTION

- This weapon is very powerful and useful when collaboration is used
- Its power is evident when used daily
- Be a real leader and apply this weapon consistently in your school

Chapter 4

A Day Late and a Buck Short

"Always train in a vibrant and joyful manner."
Morihei Ueshiba

Preparing to Teach

"Always train in a vibrant and joyful manner," is a quote by Morihei Ueshiba, the founder of aikido. He is referred to as *O'Sensei*, which means "Great teacher" (Saotome and Ikeda, Third Edition, 2). His quote inspired me to develop the weapons for teachers in this chapter.

Aikido is a defensive martial art that uses rolls, throws, falls and holds to neutralize an attacker. It is physically, emotionally and intellectually demanding. There is a significant amount of physical discomfort when you are the attacker and the defensive techniques are being applied to you. Therefore, if you can't "Train in a vibrant and joyful manner," as is suggested above, the pain associated with training can force you to quit.

We need to embrace the teaching profession in the same manner. As teachers, we want to be successful and work in a vibrant and joyful manner. However, many dedicated teachers experience emotional pain on a regular basis. This can temper their vibrancy and joy.

ENOUGH IS ENOUGH

In being a true professional, it's a given that teachers be thoroughly prepared each day. We put a great deal of time and energy into preparing and planning what methods to use in teaching the subject matter. However, there are other important areas that often go unattended, until a point is reached when we may say "Enough is enough."

I reached that point on a cold and rainy Monday morning, after being up half the night correcting tests and oversleeping. Gathering the corrected tests, and other teaching materials, I scrambled for something to wear. While having a quick bite to eat, it was off to the car, with coffee and tests in hand. Looking in the back seat, I noticed my umbrella was missing and realized my teenage daughter must have borrowed it. There was no time to look for another one.

On the way to school, I noticed that the car's gas gauge was on "E," that doesn't mean "Enough!" The clock was ticking as I quickly stopped at the gas station. After getting every red light possible, and finally pulling into the high school parking lot, sure enough, my assigned parking space was taken. I pulled into a space at the far end of the lot and ran into school soaking wet, with corrected papers dripping in my hand.

The principal was waiting at the door, and made a chastising comment as I darted to my homeroom. The students were lined up outside the room and I asked for their help, while fumbling to find the key. No question about it, I was "A day late and a buck short!" These events had a negative affect on me for the rest of the day. It didn't matter how well prepared I was methodologically or subject-wise, everything seemed to be more challenging than normal.

By the end of that day, I made a decision never to be late for work again. The principal will never see an image of me as a disheveled teacher, because the "absent-minded professor" look is never in vogue. The students will never get a damp, wrinkled test paper returned to them. Lastly, no matter what the circumstances, I will always project a professional image.

TEACHER DAILY PREPAREDNESS

It was time to develop a routine that would allow me to be thoroughly prepared each day. This routine should only take a minimal amount of time and effort in the morning. Logically, my preparation should be done at night. It was time to begin a new routine. My clothes were selected, pressed and placed in a designated area of the closet. My neckties were tied and placed on a hanger with each shirt. The gas tank was not allowed to fall below the ¼ mark. A briefcase was purchased to protect my teaching materials. This is not a frill. Tests and grades are confidential, and need to be secure and in good order. My lunch was made in the evening and stored in the refrigerator, so it can quickly be grabbed in the morning. The brief case was placed in the car each night.

Lastly, getting up a little earlier each morning allowed me more time to leisurely and safely get to work. By telling myself, "This is something that I *have* to do," instead of something I *should* do, it became an empowering habit and a powerful teacher weapon.

HIGH STANDARD IN THE DOJO

In martial arts, the *dojo* has very high standards for neatness, cleanliness, personal hygiene and organization. Everything has a designated place. There is a specific place for visitors, a dressing area, and a workout (*tatami mat*) area. There are procedures to follow to keep the *dojo* clean before and after class. Cleanliness and organization shows respect for the martial art and its participants.

HIGH STANDARD IN THE CLASSROOM

If there is a high standard of organization and cleanliness in the *dojo*, shouldn't we strive to attain the same standard in our classroom? It is essential to have this standard. If we expect our students to achieve high standards, it is critical for our classrooms to be clean, neat and organized. A clean and well-organized environment benefits both the teacher and the students, by creating a positive teaching and learning environment.

In each classroom, students and teacher must work each day to keep things neat and organized. It is the teacher's responsibility to organize or discard any outdated textbooks, resources, answer keys and old test papers. Good organization saves time.

As professionals, we must try not to hoard and keep unnecessary materials. Begin to develop a system of sorting and reorganizing materials at the beginning, middle and end of each year. Donate any materials you do not need, give them to another teacher or throw them away. The basic rule is if it hasn't been used in three years, it's time to get rid of it. Managing materials is an important teacher weapon that must be used to fight clutter and create organization. This weapon can eliminate the stress involved in trying to find things in an unorganized room.

In conclusion, half-hearted efforts in daily preparation and managing teaching resources will lead us to half-hearted results. So let's get organized, and enable ourselves to be vibrant, joyful and enthusiastic teachers.

Just a Thought ...

Make sure today's activities are purposeful and well planned.

Chapter 4 - Teacher Weapons Review

WEAPON: TEACHER DAILY PREPAREDNESS

- Get clothes together at night and place in an easily accessible location
- Fill up vehicle's gas tank the previous night
- Obtain carrying case to transport teaching materials
- Place items for work in car the night before
- Give yourself plenty of time to get to work
- Tell yourself, "This is something that I have to do"

WEAPON: MANAGING OUR TEACHING ACCUMULATIONS

- Fight the clutter and get organized
- Weed out accumulations three times a year
- Use the three-year rule to determine what to keep
- Stop hoarding and keeping everything
- Remember, there's less stress when there's no mess

Chapter 5

Are You Coming Down with a Bug? Or Is Your Job Bugging You?

"Life is not to live, but to be well."

Martial
(The Epigrams of Martial)

The Joy of Teaching

Are you coming down with a bug or is your job bugging you? There was a time in my teaching career that I asked myself this question. It was very instrumental in helping me and some of my colleagues.

Most teachers really enjoy their profession and get a great deal of satisfaction in helping students learn. However what really seems to bug teachers comes under what I refer to as the "non-teaching" category. This category attacks us from many different angles and impedes our efforts to teach. It can frustrate and drain us of our energy.

Included in this category are the frequent classroom interruptions. These may come from the public address announcements, answering of the classroom phone and the unscheduled visits to the classroom. Some days are better than others; however, these interruptions can really get out of control.

Also included in this category is the plethora of tasks that are stuffed into our school mailboxes. I'm sure you could add your own items to this "non-teaching" category. At times, teachers may feel they're being attacked by so many "non-teaching" items that at the end of the day they're emotionally drained.

By asking, "Am I coming down with a bug or is this job bugging me?" you may come to the realization that you need help to effectively deal with these challenges. There is no doubt about it, dealing with these non-teaching tasks and interruptions can be frustrating and overwhelming. Why? Because they are only indirectly related to actually teaching and take so much of our time and energy.

Over a long period of time, this can take a real toll on our emotional and physical health. It can cause teachers to miss work. Teacher absences from school are educationally hurting our students and financially expensive to the school district. So, how can we spell relief? *RANDORI*

RANDORI

In martial arts, *randori* (Japanese) is when several people, usually three to five, surround and attack a defender. This barrage is continued until the attackers are subdued or the defender is defeated. The attackers can use weapons, while the defender must begin unarmed.

Obviously this type of training is practiced by the more advanced martial artists, since it is a very intense activity and is performed at a very fast pace. *Randori* tests the limits of a defender's skill, body and mind. The defender can easily feel overwhelmed, fearful, and even be panic stricken.

I had similar experiences as a teacher, when I was attacked with problems, interruptions, and difficult situations. This is known as *"teacher randori."* Training in martial arts *randori* helped me to develop weapons that could be used in teacher *randori*.

PRIORITIZE

A defender in martial arts *randori* must quickly prioritize the attackers and the defensive techniques that will be used. This prioritization will depend on the attackers' proximity, speed and type of attack, whether or not they are armed, as well as their size.

This split-second prioritization process will continue throughout the *randori*. It is very obvious that hesitation and procrastination are not viable options. So how does this translate into the classroom?

There were days as a teacher that I worked very hard and yet felt unfulfilled. This was so, because I was working on things that I didn't consider important. Why did this happen? It happened because I wasn't prioritizing. As educators, we need to work hard, but we must also work smart.

Previous to this discovery, it was normal to drop whatever I was doing to help colleagues and staff members. Many times these people were in a panic-stricken state. They either procrastinated on a task that an administrator gave them and was due right away or didn't do enough planning and needed immediate help. A great majority of these interruptions were bailouts that could have easily been avoided.

By setting daily priorities and not being as easily available to others, my real responsibilities as a teacher came to the forefront. A belief was quickly developed that poor planning by another person does not constitute an emergency for me. In other words, I have no reservations in helping anyone, but it needs to be done at a time that also works for me. This approach helped me and also helped the procrastinators, who stopped expecting a bailout. In the end, there was a healthier working relationship. Prioritization gave the hard work more meaning.

Another benefit was derived surprisingly from prioritizing daily. There were days when I was not up to handling some of the very difficult problems that were next on the priority list. I discovered that shifting my focus to tackling smaller problems increased my confidence and energy. It enabled me to be in a better state of mind to handle the more difficult situations.

Another discovery was made when using a technique in martial arts *randori*. The approach is for the defender to throw a larger attacker at other attackers. The larger attacker will impede the other attackers' efforts and timing. By applying this same approach to teaching, in the process of solving a bigger problem, I found that some of the smaller problems would also be solved. Start to prioritize daily and you may see some awesome benefits, too.

MAKE A DECISION AND TAKE IMMEDIATE ACTION

Randori shows the importance of prioritizing and the benefits that come along with it. It also brought out the importance of not delaying in making decisions and immediately taking the appropriate action. A defender in martial arts *randori* can't waste any time in deciding how to respond to the ongoing attacks. Hesitation and procrastination are not viable options.

This is also true of teachers. Making decisions and taking the immediate appropriate action can be a very powerful weapon. The decisions we make and actions we take determine how successful we think and feel about ourselves. As a result, the person you become is directly connected to the decisions and actions that you cumulatively make.

This is contrary to a popular belief that the conditions or circumstances that are encountered, determine success or failure. For example, as a defender, it is not just the circumstances that surround us, but the effectiveness of the defensive technique used that's important. How we subdue our attackers is most important.

Similarly, as teachers, we are presented with many difficult challenges that our students bring to the classroom. Making the decisions and taking the actions in teaching them is what's most important. *Randori* directs us to make decisions often and not to procrastinate. The more decisions that are made by us each day; the better we become at making them.

Occasionally a wrong decision may be made, but keep in mind, there is no one on the face of this earth who is perfect. Everyone makes mistakes. Try to learn from each mistake and move forward. This is just part of the decision-making process.

Beware of those who are quick to criticize the decisions of others. People who seem not to make mistakes are those who often do little and make few decisions. Their comments should be taken with a grain of salt.

Procrastinators, on the other hand, painfully delay making decisions. They allow their circumstances to control them. One needs to realize that not making a decision **is** a decision. Conversely, by making decisions often and taking immediate action, the problems and circumstances won't control us. So use this powerful weapon often.

MENTAL PREPARATION FOR TEST TAKING

Whenever we are experiencing *randori*, it is vital that we be in a calm state of mind. This state allows our minds to be clear and open. It elicits a feeling that we are ready for just about anything. Starting out in a calm state is a lot easier than trying to transition out of being emotionally upset. Therefore, mental preparation is extremely important. If this preparation is so important and so powerful, how can it be used in teaching and transferred to the students?

In practicing martial arts *randori*, a great deal of stress is on the defender to perform, which is very similar to the stress that students encounter while taking tests. A defender trains to remain calm and be alert by controlling their breathing pattern and maintaining a proper posture. In *randori*, a defender who doesn't remain calm gets winded very quickly and is defeated.

Keeping students calm during a test enables them to do their best. The following procedure was developed to enable students to be calm and alert when taking tests.

This procedure should be practiced several times before the date of the test. It should also be practiced just before the test is actually given to the students. Teachers should perform this procedure along with the students. There are two components to this procedure. The first is controlling our breathing pattern and the second is maintaining a proper posture.

It is very important to control the speed and pace of your breathing. Use a slow and flowing breathing pattern, not a fast, short and shallow one. Start by inhaling slowly through your nose, while expanding your belly. Hold your breath momentarily. Exhale slowly through your mouth at a slower rate than your inhale rate, while flattening your belly. The teacher and students should do this procedure in unison three to five times, consecutively.

While breathing, maintain proper posture. Chins should be up and parallel to the floor, spine straight, and shoulders down and relaxed. By following this procedure just before the actual test is given, a calm state of mind can be achieved by the students and the teacher who is administering the test. This procedure has been very effective for martial artists, students and teachers. Many students and faculty members have witnessed and experienced the power of proper breathing and posture. It is equally effective at the elementary, secondary and college levels.

In conclusion, a calm state of mind is empowering and powerful. The utilization of this procedure empowers your students to do their very best.

> *For the uncontrolled there is*
> *no wisdom*
> *For the uncontrolled*
> *no concentration.*
> *For the unconcentrated*
> *no peace.*
> *For the unpeaceful*
> *no happiness can be.*

Bhagavadgita
(Dobson T. and V. Miller 1993, 77)

Just a Thought ...

You can't have a good day with a bad attitude and you can't have a bad day with a good attitude.

Chapter 5 - Teacher Weapons Review

WEAPON: PRIORITIZE

- Set priorities on a daily basis
- Help others when it doesn't decimate your priorities
- If not up to solving difficult problems, change priorities to handle many smaller ones first
- In the process of solving difficult problems, some of the smaller problems may disappear
- Work on issues that are important to you, which may enable you to work smarter and feel fulfilled
- Take control of your time and your life

WEAPON: DON'T DELAY IN MAKING DECISIONS AND TAKING IMMEDIATE ACTION

- Make decisions often
- The more decisions that we make, the better we get at making them
- The decisions and actions that we make on a regular basis determines our success

WEAPON: MENTAL PREPARATION FOR TEST TAKING

- Control breathing pattern while maintaining a proper posture

BREATHING PATTERN

- Inhale through nose slowly, and expand belly
- Hold breath momentarily
- Exhale slowly through your mouth (slower than you inhale), while your belly flattens

PROPER POSTURE

- Chin up and parallel to the floor
- Spine straight
- Shoulders down and relaxed

Chapter 6

Transform Resistance into Assistance

"When you reach real ability you will be able to become one with the enemy. Entering his heart you will see that he is not your enemy after all."

Sword Master Tsuji

Resistance into Assistance

In the martial art of aikido, the defender uses an oncoming attack to assist him in executing his defensive technique. This is accomplished by upsetting the attacker's balance and restraining him with a painful hold or lock; which forces the attacker to give up.

Since there are numerous ways that a person may be attacked, there are equally numerous defensive techniques to use. These defensive techniques use the laws of gravity, centrifugal force and centripetal force in adapting to the attacking techniques.

It should be noted that aikido is strictly a defensive martial art. There is no aikido technique to use unless one is attacked. It is such a sophisticated martial art, that the intent is not to kill, maim or even hurt the attacker. Instead, its intent is to neutralize the attacker and make the attacker give up. This is why aikido is commonly referred to as "The art of peace." (Ueshiba 1992, 5)

In aikido, there is a very important concept regarding communication called *musubi* (Japanese). "*Musubi*, as it is refined, can mean the ability to control and alter interaction, changing a hostile approach to a healthy encounter or an attack into a handshake." (Saotome 1989, 9) In other words, *musubi* is the study of good communication.

If aikido and *musubi* can help transform a threatening and resistant situation into one of harmonious assistance, can they be utilized by teachers? The answer is yes, keeping in mind that martial artists do most of their communication in the form of actions and reactions, while teachers do a great deal of their communication through the use of the English language.

TEACHER MUSUBI

Knowing the students, having an excellent work ethic, mastering the subject matter, being an excellent communicator and possessing a rich repertoire of successful teaching techniques are major components in being an excellent teacher. However, there is another major component that needs our attention as well; this is referred to as "*teacher musubi.*" What is it? It's a teacher's sense and skill in determining **on demand** when to be flexible and adaptive in their approach and how to communicate to their students.

To attain this extraordinary ability, we need to continually develop our repertoire of methods, but more so, to develop our verbal communication skills to transform their resistance into assistance. Teacher *musubi* also deals with any encounter when resistance needs to be transformed into assistance. Teachers need weapons to help them with the power to transform. These weapons can be used in the classroom with their students. They can also be very useful when dealing with a difficult staff member, during parent conferences, and with an administrator regarding a difficult issue.

THE TRANSFORMING POWER IN WORDS

"Without knowing the force of words, it is impossible to know me," by Confucius. (Soothill 1995, 122)

The first weapon for teachers to use to transform resistance into assistance lies in the power of words. The use of the word *but* creates resistance. "Used unconsciously and automatically it can be one of the most destructive words in our language." "But" negates what preceded it. (Robbins 1987, 279)

By paying close attention to people when they use *but* in their conversations, the resistance that is created can be identified. This alerts us to be very careful not to use *but* in conversations. So what can we use in its place? According to Robbins, use the word *instead*. (Robbins 1987, 279)

For example, during a mandatory teacher development class, a colleague said, "You may not complain about these classes, but I know you hate them even more than I do." Without my colleague realizing it, he created a resistance in me by using the word *but*. Even though I agreed with what he said, I wanted to challenge him.

In this instance, it turned out to be a good thing. My

response to him was, "Instead of focusing on how much we despise these classes, let's try to improve our attitude, ask intelligent questions, and be intent listeners. Maybe we will learn something that can be immediately applied in our classrooms."

Another word that can have a negative impact in its use, is the word *whatever*, when used as a comment by itself. It's thought to be contemporary and trendy, but it is **not** a good thing. I believe using *whatever* this way is very disrespectful to the receiving person, because it has the connotation of saying, "Shut up," and "I don't want to hear any more from you."

For instance, if my only reply to my colleague at the teacher development session was, "Whatever," it would not only be disrespectful, but unprofessional as well. In other words, disrespecting people can occur on a daily basis, whether we intend to or not. This disrespect is very real and creates resistance.

So if a person uses *whatever* in that way, you can counter it by saying, "I don't understand what you mean. Can you please be more specific?" This demonstrates their comment wasn't accepted and they need to rethink what has been said.

I have come across many people who use *whatever* this way and don't realize they are being disrespectful. Realizing the power that exists in words, teachers must acknowledge their role as wordsmiths. By paying careful attention to the resistance and the negativity that the words *but* and *whatever* can create, we can transform the resistance into assistance.

Redirecting Verbal Attacks

POSITIVES VS. NEGATIVES

Words are not the only weapon that can be used to transform resistance into assistance. There are other weapons that are available to help us redirect verbal attacks into a productive and positive encounter.

Throughout my career as a teacher and a principal in an urban setting, I used weapons at numerous parent conferences. These conferences started out to be very negative, but were transformed to have a positive and collaborative tone. A very high percentage of these conferences helped establish and continue an ongoing collaboration between the school and the home.

An excellent weapon to use is to emphasize the positive aspects of an experience, while downplaying the negative ones. Please note that I am **not** saying to ignore negative situations or experiences. On the contrary, we need to work very hard and vigilantly on them. However, a sustained determination and focus needs to be set on the positive aspects, to help change the negative ones into new positive ones.

Too many people tend to get stuck on the negative aspects of a situation, especially when they are currently experiencing very difficult circumstances. They take for granted all the hard work that went into making several other aspects successful. This can be especially true during parent conferences involving a student's poor academics or misbehavior.

For example, one of my students had to be suspended from school for fighting in the hallway. Having been involved in breaking up the fight, my attendance was necessary at the principal's hearing. The student's father was very angry throughout the hearing. He was not happy that he had to take time off from work.

At the conclusion of the hearing, I approached this parent and asked him to meet with me privately for no more than 10 minutes. Surprisingly, he agreed. In that brief time, I told him that although his son had made a serious mistake, he was working very hard and doing well in my advanced accounting class. Furthermore, his son had intentions of pursuing a career to become a Certified Public Accountant (CPA).

Although this suspension may be a speed bump in his high school education, I emphasized that we shouldn't lose sight of his son's long-term goal. The conference ended by thanking him for his time under such difficult circumstances. This quick conference quieted down the parent and gave him something important and positive to focus on, other than the consequences of his son's behavior.

At the end of the marking period, it was a pleasant surprise to see that this parent attend his son's conference, as he had missed the one earlier in the year. He was thankful that our previous conversation helped him properly discipline his son, and support his career goals.

Overall, it improved communication at home. The parent thanked me for breaking up the fight before anyone was seriously hurt. In the end, the parent's verbal attacks were truly redirected. Ultimately, his son became an accomplished CPA.

There were many other instances when this weapon was used; however, this 10-minute conference proved to be one of the shortest and quickest in redirecting a very strong verbal attack.

Transforming Resistance into Assistance during Difficult Conferences

In the martial art of aikido, when attacked, a defender uses either an *irimi* (Japanese) or a *tenkan* (Japanese) as a **first** defensive move. An *irimi* is an entering move, while a *tenkan* is a turn.

These moves place the defender in very close proximity to the attacker and at a very advantageous angle and really embrace the onset of an oncoming attack in its earliest stage. They do not wait for the attack to be fully executed. There cannot be any delay or hesitation in performing either of these defensive moves.

Similarly, when a teacher sees a difficult situation forming, it should be handled in a similar fashion. Instead of performing an *irimi* or a *tenkan*, there should be no delay or hesitation in setting up a conference. When making the initial contacts to arrange the conference, respect, along with an open mind, needs to be consistently practiced.

In other words, one must always respect and never denigrate, no matter how emotional anyone may get. Certain tactics can be helpful in achieving this. For example, when setting up a conference and someone starts to go *ballistic* on the phone, respectfully interrupt.

This interruption could be, "Excuse me, I am very interested in what you have to say, so get your thoughts organized and ready for the upcoming conference. I want to fully understand what you have to say, so that we can all work together to improve the situation." This posturing notifies the participants that we all should be intent listeners and strive to collaborate in improving the situation.

When the conference begins, the introductions are made respectfully and politely. Before each person has a turn in stating his/her side of the situation, it must be made clear that everyone's comments are important and need to be heard respectfully. You should monitor this process closely and employ certain weapons immediately, if the discussion takes a negative turn.

If the conversation during the conference starts to get emotionally charged, respond by speaking at a pronounced slower rate. By speaking deliberately, the intensity of their emotions will decrease. At the same time, it is also important to speak confidently, whether we feel confident or not. Both of these tactics foster less impulsive comments and promote more reflective ones.

Respectful interruptions are other powerful weapons that can be used to bring a ranting and emotional outburst to a screeching halt. It forces one to stop and think. An example would be to interrupt by asking clarifying questions to what was said. These questions can be used especially when someone starts to get emotional. Like a defensive move in aikido, don't allow your attack to be fully executed. Asking clarifying and open-ended questions in a respectful manner can be an awesome and powerful weapon.

Another weapon that can be used to interrupt a parent, who becomes emotionally charged, is to have them restate what they mean, but **slowly**. When you interrupt them, explain that you really want to **completely** understand what they have to say. Continue to respectfully interrupt them whenever they seem to pick up negative emotional momentum. This will enable them to slow down and help them think before they speak.

Lastly, another weapon that can be used, when appropriate, is a humorous comment or pun, but must be used with good judgment. (Robbins 1987, 286) It must **never** be hurtful. If you question, whether you should use it or not, don't. It's better to be safe than sorry with this one; however, it has served me well.

By tactically interrupting emotionally-charged discussions, you will enable the conference to progress steadily and successfully. By listening intently, asking quality questions, using facts and the information that was stated at this conference, you can view the situation comprehensively. This allows you to ascertain and focus on the underlying cause.

The symptoms that were getting a great deal of the attention can now be pushed aside. The situation can be redefined, which clears the way for a solution, because of everyone's effort and input. In addition, since collaboration was a major part in this conference, future collaboration becomes a cinch, by simply including a plan that handles any future incidents. I have repeatedly experienced success throughout my career as an educator following this process and using these weapons.

This conferencing process involves investigation, elaboration and collaboration. Investigation includes making the contacts in setting up and starting the conference. Elaboration is using all the facts and information from the conference and redefining the situation, thereby arriving at a clear solution. Collaboration was used throughout this entire conferencing process. So don't hesitate to investigate, elaborate and collaborate to transform resistance into assistance when conferencing.

Just a Thought ...

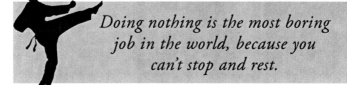

Doing nothing is the most boring job in the world, because you can't stop and rest.

Chapter 6 - Teacher Weapons Review

WEAPON: THE TRANSFORMING POWER IN WORDS

- The word *but* creates resistance and can be very destructive, because it negates the words previous to it
- Replace the word *but* with *instead*
- The word *whatever*, when used by itself as a comment, creates resistance

WEAPON: EMPHASIZE THE POSITIVE ASPECTS AND DOWNPLAY THE NEGATIVE ONES

- Work at changing negative aspects into becoming our new positive ones
- Too many people get stuck on the negative aspects of a situation, especially when they are in a difficult situation
- Don't take for granted all the hard work that goes into making all the other aspects of a situation positive
- Negative statements imply hopelessness, while positive statements imply hopefulness

WEAPON: TRANSFORMING RESISTANCE INTO ASSISTANCE DURING DIFFICULT CONFERENCES

- Don't delay or hesitate in setting up a conference when a difficult situation is forming
- Keep an open mind throughout the conferencing process
- Respect and never denigrate, no matter how emotional a person becomes
- Respectfully interrupt each time an incident gets highly emotional by using the following:
- Ask clarifying questions
- Speak slowly
- Have the person **slowly** restate their concern
- Use humor appropriately
- Redefine the situation by using the facts and information derived from the conference
- Arrive at a clear solution
- Include a plan on how to handle any future incidents
- Involve investigation, elaboration and collaboration in the conferencing process

Chapter 7

Transform Your Toughest Foe into Your Biggest Ally: Take the Worry Out of High-Stakes Testing

"He who knows much about others may be learned, but he who understands himself is more intelligent. He who controls others may be powerful, but he who has mastered himself is mightier still."

Lao Tsu, Tao Teb King
(The Art of War)

High-Stakes Testing

Let's start by defining high-stakes tests. They are any federal, state, and/or standardized tests that are administered to students. Their scores are used to evaluate the academic performance of the students, teachers, school, school district and state. The results of these tests are used to compare and point out the disparities in all of the above categories. Some states use these tests in determining the allotment of financial funding to the schools and their districts. This can place a great deal of pressure on everyone. They know they must do well on the tests or deal with the consequences, hence, the term high-stakes testing.

It is, therefore, important for our teachers to take the worry out of high-stakes testing so that students will be able to perform well on the tests. However, there are two components **teachers** need to examine and work on, before this can take place. These components are: fighting yourself by beginning a cycle of self-mugging, and defending you from yourself.

Once these components have been successfully dealt with, and you have transformed your toughest foe into your biggest ally, then you can utilize the eight-step teaching paradigm that is presented later in this chapter. By working on the two components first and then using the teaching paradigm, it will serve as a one-two blow in attacking high-stakes tests.

Fighting Ourselves

When training in martial arts, the most difficult challenge is not the attacker in front of us; rather, it is the fighting that is going on internally. How well or how poorly we deal with this internal fighting is reflected in our performance. Don't be fooled into thinking that because we may not be aware of what is going on internally, that it will not have any effect on us. On the contrary, what we don't know can and does affect us. This cognition helped me realize that we can either be our toughest foe or our biggest ally. This applies to us whether we are teaching in the classroom or training in martial arts.

Furthermore, Dobson and Miller suggest that "We are our own most hostile aggressor as well as the victim of our own hostility. In an average day most human beings attack themselves at least once an hour." (Dobson and Miller 1993, 79) We do this by internally belittling ourselves, using every reason possible.

This may start from the moment that we get out of bed and start attacking our body image. We may continue this barrage by aiming at some of our character traits or abilities. There is no doubt that every day we have many internal "muggings" that invariably go undefended and unresolved. (Dobson and Miller 1993, 79) I believe by not confronting these muggings, the cycle of self-mugging will continue.

As a teacher, you have a great deal of students, problems and issues that keep your mind occupied with worry and anxiety. What is at the top of your worry and anxiety list? You spend more time with yourself than with anyone else. Therefore, it is critical that you pay close attention to how you talk to yourself, how it affects you, and how you defend yourself. A weapon is needed to defend you from yourself because you can be your own WORST critic.

REPLACE WORRY AND ANXIETY WITH ACTION AND SATISFACTION

Replacing worry and anxiety with action and satisfaction is a weapon that can be used against the two important above-mentioned components that teachers need to confront. Because we can be so brutal when we fight ourselves, we need powerful and positive weapons to help us.

While driving to a martial arts class one day, I started to think "I hope that I don't get hurt tonight." This continued for two months, each time I drove to the *dojo*. Upon questioning this state of mind, the answer was clear. Worrying was feeding the fear in me, and I started to doubt my abilities. In essence, a problem was being fabricated that was sucking the enjoyment out of my martial arts training.

These thoughts were a useless **waste** of time and energy. By continuing to do this, I was allowing myself to be nothing more than a trash receptacle full of worry and anxiety. All this worry and anxiety was enabling me to be a **basket** case! This comical but logical conclusion helped me reach a point to stop this self-destructive thinking. By quickly replacing, "I hope that I don't get hurt tonight in the dojo," with, "I'm excited about learning a new technique in class," I learned to relax and enjoy the workout. Thoughts of worry and anxiety were simply replaced with action and satisfaction.

This was the birth of a useful weapon that can be used when dealing with the difficult and worrisome issue of high-stakes testing. It's an issue that can emotionally drain you, and everyone in the school. This weapon can defend you from yourself and extinguish your worry and anxiety.

START DEFENDING YOURSELF

Defending you from yourself is the other component that needs every teacher's attention. After being hired as a high school teacher in a New York State urban public school, it was clearly expressed to me that my evaluation would largely consist of the students' performance on the state tests, and their behavior in the classroom. Next year's contract depended on these factors.

The teacher, who held this position before me, was let go because of poor performance in both these areas. I understood what was expected of me. From my perspective, this upped the ante on the high-stakes testing. Many other teachers were in this same situation. Teachers frequently expressed their worry and anxiety about how their students would perform on the tests. They commented that students increasingly have more and more educational needs.

In addition to the daily informal discussions, this topic was found on the agenda at every faculty meeting. It became a concern throughout the school, and there seemed to be no respite in sight. A superficial effort on the part of an administrator would periodically be made to reassure teachers. A comment would be, "Don't worry **so much** about these state tests." This statement was no help to us, because it couldn't camouflage our obvious worry and concern. Whenever someone made a comment about the state tests, it triggered a plethora of negative thoughts.

I came to realize that I was responsible for emotionally beating myself up with this stinking thinking. It really doesn't matter what other people are saying—it is how it's being handled internally that's important. Therefore, the students and teachers need to defend themselves against the negative thoughts associated with testing. Keeping in mind the weapons learned in martial arts, it was now time for us to replace worry and anxiety with action and satisfaction. It's not what you do that counts, but what you get done.

Each class period should be viewed and treated in the same manner as the training sessions held in martial arts. Every minute of class time should be viewed as precious and important. The students and teacher must realize that each class is one piece of a 190-piece puzzle (190 represents the number of days in the school year). If everyone in the class-room is as serious and hard working as the people in the dojo, positive results on the tests can be achieved.

However, we can't think that merely talking to the students about this approach is all that's needed. Instead, you must thoroughly convince the students that you will provide them with exceptional teaching and effort on a daily basis. In return, students need to show cooperation, be thoroughly prepared for class, and give exceptional effort each day.

These actions will ensure success and promote the feeling of satisfaction. It will begin to silence the negative thoughts of high-stakes testing. The next step is to use the eight-step teaching paradigm, which will prepare and ready the students for the high-stakes tests.

EIGHT-STEP TEACHING PARADIGM

I wanted to ensure that my dedication, commitment and hard work as a teacher was maximized in helping students do their very best. It became obvious that I needed to make some comprehensive changes in the way I operated and taught throughout the day. After comparing where my students presently were, academically, and where they need-ed to be by the end of the school year, I realized a great deal of work needed to be done.

The following eight-step teaching paradigm was used, which enabled me to experience a great deal of success. This includes the areas of test data analysis suggested in, *A Guide For Implementing Total Quality Management And Effective Schools Research*, by Bill Rauhauser, Ph.D. Those areas are: prerequisite skills, materials, time, timing

format, vocabulary, objectives and methodology.
(Rauhauser unpublished, 103)

1. The teacher's planning and preparation needs to be three-dimensional. It has greater specificity, short and long-term goals/objectives, and is within the teacher-developed timeline for this subject. This planning and preparation includes the advanced organizers of the subject matter, and any anticipated student misbehaviors.

2. The teaching methodologies for each class include alternative and adaptive approaches that can be aligned to each student's strengths and weaknesses because 25% of the students learn by hearing, 30% by seeing and 45% by doing.

3. An exceptional use of class time has to be followed every day. Academic learning is the target, not the time allocated or engaged in instruction.

4. The teacher needs to consistently pursue the most effective methods including utilizing colleagues, teaching colleges, state education department, and research.

5. The teacher consistently must be available to the students before, after and during the school day, whenever possible. Consistently being available to the students is a huge benefit.

6. The teacher performs an item analysis on each test that is given to help designate the weak content areas that may need to be taught again.

7. Show the students how they can do a test analysis on their own individual tests or quizzes. This helps them know why they put down an incorrect answer.

It increases their depth of subject matter and improves their analytical skills.

8. The teacher should provide an immediate and personal notification to individuals such as the student's parent, coach, or advisor, when they become deficient on class work, homework, cooperation, and test preparedness. A reminder of the teacher's accessibility to the students should also be made at this time.

Following this eight-step teaching paradigm enabled my students to experience great success on the state tests. It replaced thoughts of worry and anxiety with action and satisfaction. However, the eight steps in this paradigm took a tremendous amount of time, hard work and energy. There were too many days when I came home from teaching and felt totally drained. My tank was on empty and I had very little teaching endurance.

A different series of negative thoughts started to dominate my thinking. These thoughts included, "This eight-step paradigm is too hard. You're crazy working so hard every day. Nobody works this hard day-after-day." A weapon was needed to defend myself from these thoughts and help improve my teaching endurance. The following martial arts concepts would help develop this much-needed teacher weapon.

KEEPING BALANCE AND CENTER BY NOT OVERTRAINING

In the martial art of aikido, our *hara* (Japanese) is the starting point for all movement. It is referred to as one's center of gravity, and is located in the lower abdomen, approximately two inches below the belly button. This knowledge is important for us to use in keeping our balance; it's also referred to as our center.

Martial artists have been studying the art of balance for many years. Its study is not only used to increase physical skills, but to help them meet life and its challenges. Having balance allows martial artists to be alert, relaxed and completely focused. (Dobson and Miller 1993, 79) A martial artist cannot afford to be off-balance, because being anxious or hysterical can steal your center and balance.

Teaching can totally deplete your energy and knock you off balance. Martial artists call it giving up their "center." True martial artists strive to stay in balance and teachers should strive to do the same. But how can one be in balance as a teacher and still be successful in the classroom? This train of thought was brought to the forefront at a time when I was injured in Aikido and unable to train for several months.

I normally train in martial arts three or four times a week. However, there were times when I trained six or seven days a week, when training to take a promotional test. You may have guessed what happened next; I got injured.

By stopping the training at this time, the test was deferred for one year. Being injured was a major setback physically, but was an even bigger challenge mentally and emotionally.

Although it is important to train hard and be thoroughly prepared for a promotional test, it is extremely important to train smart and not overtrain. It was very similar to what I experienced as a teacher. Instead of overtraining, I was over-teaching. In my zeal to be an exceptional teacher, this caused me to lose my endurance. A weapon was needed to stop over-teaching, silence the negative thoughts, and restore teaching endurance.

MODERATION WITH DISCRETION FOR TEACHERS

Just like there's a need to train smarter, not harder in martial arts, the same holds true for teachers. The weapon, *moderation with discretion* is an excellent defensive weapon. It helps maintain one's balance and center by setting a proper pace throughout the school day.

Teaching is very demanding mentally, emotionally and, yes, physically. It is very rare to see a teacher sitting during class time. Most of the time, they're on their feet presenting, lecturing, helping small groups of students and giving individual instruction. In other words, one teacher on their feet is worth two in their seats!

Mentally and emotionally, teaching requires a great deal of energy. A teacher needs to continuously concentrate on the subject matter while managing the students' behavior. By staying within the boundaries of moderation with discretion, more can be accomplished each day. You need to continuously monitor and manage your teaching so that you don't **over-teach**.

Giving over-the-top presentations and being overly enthusiastic, without taking a break, can be counterproductive. Moderation with discretion in the classroom means there should be a high intensity and high enthusiasm level at a predetermined and well-planned part of a lesson. It should not last an entire class period. Developing endurance can bring teaching to a higher level.

Using moderation with discretion in the classroom also

puts students in a higher interest mode. It keeps students in suspense, as they wonder when the highest level of intensity and enthusiasm will occur.

Sometimes it may be in the middle of class, other times at the end, and still others in the beginning. This brings a new level of interest to each class. It also adds a new dimension to teacher creativity, and makes negative thoughts disappear.

As a result of using the teacher weapons discussed in this chapter, the students and I experienced great success on the state tests. High-stakes testing needs to be dealt with effectively, so that the classroom and the entire school can have a successful and enjoyable educational atmosphere.

Just a Thought ...

Worry is like sitting in a rocking chair. It accomplishes nothing, but does give you something to do.

Chapter 7 - Teacher Weapons Review

WEAPON: REPLACE WORRY AND ANXIETY WITH ACTION AND SATISFACTION

- Transform your toughest foe into your biggest ally by working on two components:
- Fighting yourself with the cycle of self-mugging
- Defending you from yourself

WEAPON: VIEW EVERY MINUTE OF CLASS TIME AS PRECIOUS AND IMPORTANT

- Universal view that each class period is one piece of a 190-piece puzzle (190 days in a school year)
- Teacher provides exceptional teaching and effort
- Students give exceptional cooperation, test preparedness and effort

WEAPON: EIGHT-STEP TEACHING PARADIGM

1. Teacher's planning and preparation has specificity, short- and long-term goals/objectives, is within the teacher developed timeline, includes the advanced organizers of the subject content, and plans for the anticipated student misbehaviors
2. Teaching methodologies are aligned to students' strengths and weaknesses
3. Exceptional use is made of class time
4. Teacher pursues the most effective methods
5. Teacher is available before, after and during the school day
6. Teacher uses item analysis on each test to help designate

the weak student content areas (materials, time, timing, format, vocabulary, objectives, methodology and prerequisite skills)

7. Teacher shows students how to do a student test analysis on each test and quiz to answer the why's to their incorrect answers

8. Teacher immediately and personally notifies individuals such, as parents and coaches, when students start to slack off

WEAPON: KEEPING YOUR BALANCE AND CENTER BY NOT OVERTRAINING OR OVER-TEACHING

WEAPON: MODERATION WITH DISCRETION FOR TEACHERS

- Use high intensity and enthusiasm at a pre-determined and well-planned part of each lesson
- This ensures teaching endurance and places the students in a higher interest mode by anticipating when the intensity and enthusiasm will be elevated

Chapter 8

I'm Not Gonna Lie to You: This Is Really Gonna Hurt!

"True victory is self-victory;
let that day arrive quickly."

Morihei Ueshiba
(O'Sensei)

The Path to This Important Chapter

This chapter covers an extremely important and demanding topic that is rarely discussed. Because this topic was not mentioned or covered at any conference, teacher development program or taught in any of my college courses, it is not surprising that the teacher weapons contained in this chapter took me years to develop. This topic was unveiled in my quest to improve overall as an educator in the following five areas:

1. Striving to attain an exemplary level of educational performance

2. Being happier when dealing with all the stresses in school

3. Consistently contributing to a positive educational atmosphere

4. Attaining and maintaining a supply of personal energy that's rechargeable and available for the next day's use

5. Maintaining an enthusiastic endurance that promotes professional success and longevity

It became apparent to me that I needed help to further advance in these five areas. I had reached a plateau and more effort on my part wasn't going to do it. The subject matter at many staff development programs sponsored by the school district seemed to be a waste of time, energy and district money.

These programs were not addressing the major concerns or dealing with the frustration that many teachers were experiencing. There were teachers, principals and other administrators who verbalized they did not know how to further improve on the gains that were already made in their schools. They believed they gave their best effort and could do no more.

However, there were others who were not satisfied in staying at a status quo level, and especially did not want to lose ground on the gains they made. No one seemed to know how to proceed. Doing more of the same would be exhausting and not produce the desired results.

Please don't misunderstand my conveyance. As a school and school district, we were performing fairly well; however, we wanted to bring it up to a higher level. This marked the beginning of my pursuit to find the missing piece.

Although many teachers gave up on their pursuit, they continued to work extremely hard, but were doing the same thing. I'm very thankful that I didn't just acquiesce, but pursued vigorously to find the topic and develop the teacher weapons that would lead to success. The use of these teacher weapons and their effectiveness should be an instantaneous process. Compare this to the years that it took to search, find and develop them.

However, there are a few things to keep in mind in utilizing the teacher weapons in this chapter. Be diligent in giving each weapon your full attention and exercise perseverance in their execution. The benefits will be well worth it.

It will provide a new consciousness and focus. It will enhance the level of enjoyment, satisfaction and overall performance. There are far too many teachers and administrators who are clueless to these weapons or even its target topic. Both are very valuable.

So what enabled me to discover this elusive topic and develop the corresponding teacher weapons? You guessed it; my experiences in martial arts.

Ukemi

Ukemi (Japanese) is pronounced (oo-kem-me). It is the part in martial arts, when an attacker receives a defensive technique, and falls or rolls unharmed. *Ukemi* is a sub-art of a martial art. A fall can be in the form of a roll, a low fall or a dangerously high fall. A high fall is also referred to as a hard fall or a break fall. Falling and rolling without getting hurt, takes a great deal of practice.

Especially in the beginning, these training sessions leaves the practitioner very sore. Extreme care must be exercised, because it is so easy to get seriously injured. Becoming proficient in taking *ukemi* requires perseverance in overcoming one's fear of the pain in falling and the possibility of injury.

I am not going to lie to you—at times it can really hurt, especially in taking high falls. However, proper training in taking *ukemi* helps both the attacker and defender. The defender is able to practice their defensive techniques on the attacker, and the attacker is able to practice *ukemi*. Since the attacker is on the receiving end of a defensive technique, it sends body clues to the attacker on how to improve the technique when they become the defender. *Ukemi* **strongly** reminds us to stay humble, especially when it becomes necessary to do a hard fall. Ouch!

PLATEAUING

Skills in performing martial arts *ukemi* reach a point where one no longer is improving, it doesn't matter how hard or how often one goes to class. This is similar to what I was experiencing professionally. This is referred to as *plateauing*. I was eager for a breakthrough to take place either in martial arts or in teaching.

In martial arts, my *sensei* (teacher) taught and helped us in our training struggles. On approaching him about the lack of progress in my *ukemi,* he said that my mind reached a point where it became closed to *ukemi*. My *ukemi* mindset needed to be changed, and I needed to empty some of the ego that accumulated in my attitude.

This emptying of attitude is a normal process in martial arts, and needs to be done often by everyone. Training hard physically is one part of martial arts. Training even harder on our attitude and character is what martial arts is really about. By respectfully listening to everything my *sensei* said, there was disappointment that he didn't give suggestions on how to physically improve my *ukemi*. This advice didn't seem to help.

Why did he say that I had to work on my attitude? I am not like some of the other people in here who brag or think they are better than everyone else. I do very little talking in the dojo, and am very attentive and focused when the instruction is given. I respectfully bow and kneel. I do more than my fair share of the cleaning in the *dojo* and am especially respectful to my defenders and attackers. Maybe *sensei* is mixing me up with somebody else or he just doesn't want to spend any more of his time on helping me with *ukemi* techniques.

Several months later, I visited a book store and was skimming through an aikido book. Three quotes that were read that day changed my life forever.

The first quote was, *"If there is a serious flaw in the personality or spiritual attitude that cannot be corrected, no matter how strong or good the technique, the finished creation will be weak and flawed."* (Saotome 1993, 134)

The second quote was; *"We must empty ourselves of ego, for ego is the boundary that sets limits on the human spirit."* (Saotome 1993, 52)

The third quote was; *"If a cup is always full, the water becomes stale and spoils. To be refreshed, it must first be emptied."* (Saotome 1993, 134)

After reading these quotations, I realized that *sensei* was not getting me mixed up with anyone else, nor that he didn't want to spend any more of his time in helping me with my *ukemi* techniques. What *sensei* said a few months ago suddenly made a great deal of sense.

My attitude was definitely in the way of my *ukemi*. It was evident in my lame thinking and excuses that I had a case of stinking thinking. He was **not** saying that I was boastful, disrespectful, not trying, or thinking of just myself. Instead, he was saying that **everyone** has to work on emptying themselves of ego.

We are unaware of how we are constantly taking small amounts of our ego and pouring it into our attitude. As our attitude starts to receive and fill up with ego, limitations are put on what we can accomplish. Because some attend to their ego daily, it is much harder for their attitude to reach a level of selfishness. On the other hand, others may stay near the full level, because they seldom attend to it.

ESCAPING OFF THE PLATEAU

The following statements are derived from the above quotations:

- If our attitude is full of ego, growth will be stymied, no matter how good or strong our skills may be
- One's ego can put limits on what can be accomplished
- An attitude full of ego can be frustrating and steal our joy
- By emptying our attitude of ego, we will be refreshed and renewed
- **Everyone** has to regularly attend to their attitude being infiltrated by their ego.

These five realizations were meaningful, powerful and life changing. They gave new meaning to the comments that *sensei* made months earlier. *Sensei* gave me very good advice and I realize that now. At my next martial arts class, my *uke-*

mi techniques immediately improved. It was both astounding and liberating. *Sensei* smiled and made the comment; "I see that you managed to dissolve some of your ego that was in your attitude."

This was a breakthrough that was long in the making. This experience showed me firsthand the limitations that my ego held on me, the frustration that it produced, and the joy it took away. More importantly, by emptying my attitude of ego, the limitations that kept me prisoner seemed to immediately disappear. This enabled me to finally escape off the *ukemi* plateau and proceed to a higher level. Is this only applicable to martial arts?

THE ELUSIVE TARGET TOPIC

By working at emptying ego from my attitude, I experienced immediate success in martial arts *ukemi*. This allowed a transition from plateauing to higher level of *ukemi*. Although unaware any ego was present in my attitude, it was foremost in my *sensei's* perception. This event was instrumental in getting me off my professional plateau. The elusive target topic that I had been searching for is **managing the ego that infiltrates our attitude**.

Why has this been such a stealth topic in the field of education? It becomes obvious when we consider that teachers are very giving individuals, who dedicate their lives to teaching others. Their students' needs are placed at the top of their priority list.

So how much sense does it make to think, that teachers need to work on their egos and attitudes? It makes a great deal of sense, when we consider *sensei's* comments and perception. Everyone needs to work on their egos, daily. There are no exemptions or exceptions. By not attending to our egos, it will continually pour into our attitudes. This limits what we can accomplish. There is no doubt that it is obligatory for everyone to continuously attend to their egos. This knowledge gave birth to the development of *teacher ukemi*.

TEACHER UKEMI

Teacher ukemi is working to dissolve our ego that continues to leak into our attitude. We need to know what our present level of ego infiltration is to give it the proper attention.

For instance, if we daily attend to our ego and limit using "me" in our words, thoughts, and actions, we may be at a low level of ego infiltration. This will enable us to collaborate with others in solving problems. Our thinking is more flexible and adaptive, because our comfort zone is not a major focus.

On the other hand, if we attend to our ego sporadically, a medium level of ego infiltration may be reached. In this range, we unknowingly put more emphasis on "me" with our words, thoughts, and acts. Less collaboration is used in solving problems, and we become less flexible and adaptive. Frustration and aggravation take a larger part in our demeanor, and more emphasis is given to staying within our comfort zone.

If we hardly ever or never attend to our ego, it may not be long before we reach the highest level of ego infiltration. At this level, our ego becomes a selfish ego. We are egocentric. Working on our ego is an afterthought or no thought at all. There is little or no regard for others; all our concern is about "Me." Our thinking is very rigid. Real collaboration is nonexistent, while dictating becomes our preferred leadership style.

Everyone, at some time or another, has visited each level. However, the real key to success is how quickly we can transition from where we are, to the lowest level of ego infiltration. This is where our true power lies.

TEACHER WEAPONS FOR TEACHER UKEMI

An Egotism Inventory Checklist

☐ puts self over anything or anyone

☐ exaggerated opinion of self

☐ looks down at people

☐ conceited

☐ arrogant

☐ self-righteous

☐ self-centered

☐ egocentric

☐ selfish

☐ in love with self

☐ self-serving

☐ foolish & selfish pride

☐ I, I, I

☐ me, me, me

☐ narrow-minded

☐ high-minded of myself

☐ vane

☐ judgmental

☐ critical

☐ puffed up opinion of myself

☐ braggart

☐ narcissistic

☐ boastful

☐ self-important

☐ stubborn

☐ finding fault in others

☐ only wants to instruct, but not be instructed

☐ not patient with the mistake of others

☐ highly opinionated

☐ comparing myself with others

☐ has bullying tendencies

☐ being a know it all

☐ self-aggrandizing

USING AN EGO INVENTORY CHECKLIST

This checklist can successfully help to deplete ego from attitude. It contains a list of descriptors which help to:

1. Admit the faults in your ego that are currently leaking into your attitude
2. Focus on the appropriate descriptors' area
3. Take the immediate action to curb and subdue your ego

This ego inventory checklist was first utilized towards the end of the school year. Our teachers union requested that each building give them a list of priorities for use in the upcoming negotiations. Everyone's input was requested. There were meetings after school for the next several days. Very heated discussions ensued at these meetings and many of us left emotionally drained and frustrated.

Using an ego inventory checklist, a quick identification was made of my problem. I was highly opinionated at these meetings. A transformation was in order for me to talk less and become a much better listener. Verbal contributions were only made, if I had a new idea. I experienced the true power derived in using this teacher weapon. My frustration level declined and I was no longer emotionally drained.

You can use the ego inventory checklist displayed in this chapter, or use it as a starting point in developing your own. Be careful **not** to use this checklist to point out other peoples' faults; it is strictly for your own use.

I used this checklist regularly, and it helped me tremendously. However, there were times when I needed more help. This paved the way to the development of yet another teacher weapon to be used along with this one. It is called *MYOB! There Is No Real Answer Key.*

MYOB! THERE IS NO REAL ANSWER KEY

In schools, both professional and non-professional staff works side by side. Some are private about their personal and family problems, while others are not. Each year, many people experience a major crisis in their lives. It could be a staff member or a spouse who is dealing with a life-threatening illness, or the death of a close family member, just to name a few.

While dealing with life's problems, they must continue to work each day. I have witnessed many people who come to the aid of their fellow workers and friends. It was both heartwarming and powerful.

However, there are other times when a much smaller personal problem is divulged and a gossiping frenzy is started. Many unknowingly get drawn into this frenzy. They give advice, opinions and are judgmental. Arguing may ensue, and people begin to take sides.

This is the time to use the teacher weapon, MYOB (Mind Your Own Business), rather than making a bad situation worse. Before taking sides, it needs to be realized there is no real answer key to life's problems. There are too many instances when all the necessary information is not available.

If you're not sure whether the advice you give is correct or helpful, don't give it. Instead, be a good listener with a caring heart. This weapon is especially effective in the faculty room, in the hallway and in the school parking lot. Keep in mind, when you have a high level of ego infiltration, you suddenly become highly opinionated, and this can translate into giving some very poor advice. This weapon will help you to be both a good listener and a true friend.

Take a Vacation Now

Wouldn't it be great to take a vacation? This does not mean you should take a day off from school. It means recognizing and focusing on all the good things in our lives. Taking a vacation from negative thoughts can help you develop an attitude of gratitude. Take the time on a regular basis to appreciate all the positive things, both big and small.

When you get stuck on the negatives, it's time to take a vacation from stinking thinking. There are positive things that need to be relied on when a negative mindset is present.

For instance, appreciate the fact that you have a good job, while others are out of work. Embrace the newly adopted textbooks that the district has purchased, even though it creates new challenges in the classroom. Take notice when students have a good attitude and are behaving well in class. Don't hesitate to include some events that may be happening in your personal life.

For example, it could be as small as a plumbing problem that at first appeared to be costly, and turns out to be a small job. Our attitude of gratitude list can be enormous. The length of your vacation should correspond with the length of time needed for emotional recovery.

Benefits of True Power for Teachers

There are many benefits that can be derived by using the teacher weapons in this chapter. A major benefit is the ability to effectively use **real collaboration** in solving very difficult problems.

This is not a superficial collaboration; like the ones that

are pre-arranged and have a secretly-planned outcome. Those "counterfeit" collaborations are a waste of everyone's time.

For instance, a superintendent once told me that he believed in shared decision making ...he makes the decisions and then **shares** it! Real collaboration is people working together and using their strengths to make improvements in their school. This becomes an even bigger benefit when a substantial number of the teachers and staff (the critical mass) use the suggestions in this chapter.

It becomes a benefit of even larger proportion when the principal is effective at emptying his/her ego. This preferred leadership style will ultimately become real collaboration. It will enable more people to solve additional problems, and become totally committed to the needs of the school. Using personal power that comes from having a service heart shows the true power in your school.

The benefits can also be reaped by just one person using the suggestions in this chapter. Even one person can have a powerful and positive affect. You don't have to wait for anyone else to step up to the plate and make a commitment before you.

It is quite obvious that martial artists and teachers need to work on emptying egos from attitudes, if they are to discover true power. Using this true power helps us individually and helps others that come in contact with us. It keeps alive a healthy enthusiasm and attitude, that contributes to a positive educational atmosphere. This is true power which enables us to achieve an exemplary level of success, regardless of the obstacles that are placed in our path.

When true power is used by teachers, it can make such

a positive difference to so many students. However, realize that working on our egos is difficult and we need to be diligent in our efforts.

Keep in mind the following quote; "…The greatest frustration, the most exhausting demand on the spirit, is the struggle to subdue the ego …"(Saotome 1993, 54)

This quotation led to the title of this chapter; *I Am Not Gonna Lie To You; This Is Really Gonna Hurt.* However, the benefits you experience can be phenomenal, professionally, personally, and throughout your school. This is true power.

Just a Thought …

You can't direct the wind but you can adjust your sail.

Chapter 8: Teacher Weapon Review

PLATEAUING

Plateauing is wanting to progress to a higher level of performance and being unable to do so.

Escaping Off the Plateau
Five Realizations of Your Ego

1. If your attitude is full of ego, your growth will be stymied, no matter how strong your skills may be
2. Your ego puts limits on what you can accomplish
3. An attitude full of ego can frustrate you and steal your joy
4. You need to empty your attitude of your ego if you are to stay refreshed and renewed
5. Regularly attend to see if your attitude is being infiltrated by ego

TEACHER *UKEMI*

Teacher *ukemi* is working to dissolve your ego that continues to leak into your attitude. We need to know what our present level of ego infiltration is in order to give it the proper attention.

Use the Egotism Inventory Checklist on page 75 as a starting point in developing your own checklist.

Weapon: MYOB! There Is No Real Answer Key

Use this weapon in conjunction with the ego inventory checklist

Mind Your Own Business

1. Be a good listener
2. Refrain from making judgments or being critical of others
3. Beware of giving your opinion, especially if it is unsolicited
4. Beware of giving advice that may be incorrect

Weapon: Take a Vacation Now

Use this weapon in conjunction with the ego inventory checklist

- Develop an attitude of gratitude
- Develop personal power with a service heart
- Recognize and focus on all the good things
- The length of vacation (attitude of gratitude exercise) should correspond to the length of time needed for emotional recovery

Benefits of True Power for Teachers

- Healthy enthusiasm and attitude
- Positive educational atmosphere
- Attaining high success, regardless of obstacles in our path
- Obtaining **real collaboration,** the biggest benefit
- Achieving critical mass to solve the most difficult problems

Chapter 9

Oh No! Not the Timer

*"Now is the time to understand more,
so that we fear less."*

Marie Curie

Sensei's Timer

After practicing martial arts for an extended period of time, a repertoire of developed skills start to become automatic. Every minute spent in a martial arts class is now perceived as very important in the quest to add to one's arsenal. No longer is it a struggle to perform the formalized warmup exercises or know the Japanese terminology for each attacking and defensive technique. Each class contributes in a small way to our existing inventory of techniques.

Sensei organizes each training session into segments. He spends a predetermined allotment of time on each segment. It is as if he has a timer in his head that goes off to end one segment and to start another. Before the end of each class, *sensei* **strings** together the segments in the class. This stringing process is very important in helping martial artists develop the techniques naturally and effortlessly.

Injury Time Out

Although each martial arts class is carefully planned and formally carried out, injuries do occur. A lapse in judgment, a missed timed technique, or a toe caught in a *tatami* (Japanese mat) are just a few examples of some mishaps that cause injuries.

Thankfully, the timer doesn't go off for serious injuries very often. However, pain, soreness and abrasions are unfortunately a normal part of martial arts training and it's a small victory when it doesn't happen.

On the other hand, some injuries may require martial artists to take an extended timeout from training; these can last for weeks and sometimes months. Injury timeouts can be very challenging physically, but even more demanding mentally. In the healing process, one will definitely lose some of the skills that were so hard to attain, and the longer we stay away from training, the more skills we lose.

During this difficult time, we need to string an honorable attitude with being patient with ourselves. In having an honorable attitude, it is unacceptable to get upset and blame others for our misfortune, even if others are careless. You are ultimately responsible for your own safety. Finger pointing or fault finding in others is not considered to be honorable.

Stringing doesn't only apply to martial arts techniques. It is especially valuable when facing the most trying circumstances. Having an honorable attitude is more than not putting blame on others. It also includes:

- Having a positive outlook
- Showing respect in the way we talk and act

- Being sincere to ourselves and others

Practicing patience is more than just waiting for someone or something to happen. It also includes:

- Having a calm state of mind while we are waiting
- Not easily giving up on ourselves or others
- Being tolerant of others and their differences

Stringing an honorable attitude with practicing patience can be very powerful for both martial artists and teachers.

Teachers Injury Time Out

Throughout my 30 plus years in education, I have witnessed teachers who had to take an injury time out for medical reasons. Before they became ill, it seemed they were always rushing to be somewhere else. They didn't seem to ever slow down long enough to enjoy the moment. When they came to a screeching halt with their own medical emergency, there was no forewarning. The timer went off and it didn't matter where they were or what they were doing.

For some of the teachers, their medical condition became a life-changing episode. They realized they needed to make some immediate changes. This is similar to the realization that a martial artist makes when recovering from an injury and returning back to training. Adjustments need to be made in the way they train if they are to remain healthy.

Martial artists and teachers who exhibit all of the elements of an honorable attitude with patience made a remarkable recovery. After their recovery, the teachers returned to their classrooms with a renewed presence. They were better teachers and happier individuals.

On the other hand, there were teachers who had to take a medical leave of absence who lacked an honorable attitude. They complained constantly and it was obvious they felt sorry for themselves for being ill. They became easily discouraged and deflated.

Ironically, these teachers did not have the more serious medical conditions. However, they acted as if no one had to ever go through what they had to experience.

When they returned to teaching, they told everyone about their medical condition and relived all their complaints. Nothing positive was derived from their injury time out experience.

By not stringing or using the elements of an honorable attitude with patience, there was no improvement in their professional and personal development. Instead they had a martyr attitude. They were left unhappy and bitter from their experience.

Still there were other teachers who were compelled to take an injury time out for the rest of their shortened lives. Yes, we all have lost some very precious friends who were excellent teachers. I frequently reminisce about the good times, and the many contributions they made.

This book is my special dedication to the many excellent teachers who taught with honor and passed away. Their contributions truly made significant differences in their students' lives.

STRINGING

Are the elements of both an honorable attitude and patience only helpful when we have to take an injury time out? Absolutely not! If maintaining an honorable attitude along with the elements of patience can help us in very trying circumstances, their power can also be reaped during ordinary circumstances. By stringing these two weapons together each day into our methods of operation in the classroom, the response received in the short run will be good, and in the long run will be extraordinary.

The respect that you'll earn from your students, colleagues, principal and parents will truly be amazing. These teacher weapons (honorable attitude and patience) are very powerful when used in the classroom and even more powerful in your personal life.

Even after I retired from working in the public school system, the power from these weapons continued to greatly exceed the boundaries of my expectations. The individuals who showed me this phenomenal power were not martial artists or teachers. They were the people who were in an all-out fight for their lives.

EVERY DAY'S A SATURDAY

In 2005 upon retiring from education, people would ask, "How is retirement?" My answer was, "It's great and every day's a Saturday."

The preparation, duties, and responsibilities that were performed for 30 plus years in public schools were no longer on my shoulders. Getting up at 5:45 AM to go to work was no longer part of my routine.

Life was much different now. A great deal of time was now available to do what I wanted to do. Going to a restaurant for breakfast or lunch during a week day was now possible. Life seemed great and it was a style that was both foreign and pleasurable at the same time.

Two years into retirement in early December, Oh! No! The timer went off. It didn't even sound like a timer; it sounded more like an alarm. It was an injury time out for my wife of 34 years, Rose Ann.

Our three children were grown and living in different parts of the country when she was diagnosed with breast cancer. Her surgery was scheduled immediately. Every day was still a Saturday, but all of a sudden, Saturday's were not so great.

Breast cancer is a serious condition and it was the first time that Rose Ann feared for her life. As a family, the children and I were committed to giving Rose Ann all the support that she needed. Her fight became **our** fight. This was a time in our lives when stringing an honorable attitude with patience was essential.

To compound an already difficult situation, the timer went off again. It went off in the recovery room right after the surgery was completed. The surgeon informed us that the cancer was not just confined to the breast; it also infiltrated a lymph node. This would mean that Rose Ann would need to go through four months of chemotherapy, followed by 38 sessions of radiation and lastly, years of drug therapy.

In an instant, the great life that we were experiencing came to a screeching halt. Every day was still a Saturday, but now all of our time and energy would be used to fight breast cancer.

The next 12 months would bring some very big challenges. These challenges would cause us to expand and elevate our physical, mental and spiritual boundaries. At times, the demands would seem insurmountable.

A TEACHER NOW BECOMES THE STUDENT

After Rose Ann recovered from the breast surgery and rehab, she started chemotherapy. She needed to go once a week for sixteen straight weeks. She would have to deal with the side affects of chemotherapy. She had persistent nausea, vomiting, diarrhea, and lost all of her hair.

Each chemo session was three hours long and I accompanied her to every session. Entering this room for the first time was very intimidating and shocking. All the cancer patients were hooked up to the numerous intravenous drugs. Being in this chemo room transformed me into a student who was to be educated on the chemotherapy drugs, and their side effects.

I became an advanced student in the school of *martial arts of the mind* like never before. This school held class in the chemo room for the next sixteen weeks.

This was not a formal school, no formal curriculum or formal assignments; the only requirement was to attend each chemo treatment session for the allotted three hours and pay very close attention to what was happening. Being attentive in the next sixteen sessions would provide me with a profound wisdom in the advanced application in *martial arts of the mind.*

CLASS ATTENDANCE COUNTS

Initially Rose Ann didn't think that one weekly chemo-therapy session for sixteen weeks would be so bad. She was wrong. This challenge turned out to be a very large one. She was so sick after receiving the first treatment that she had to return the next day and receive intravenous fluids. Weak from dehydration, she couldn't even walk.

Frankly, I don't know how she did it. I previously had three different surgeries and experienced illness, pain and discomfort. What I went through was "Kiddyland" com-pared to what she experienced. I personally never witnessed anybody as sick as she.

However, Rose Ann seemed to have an immoveable in-ner strength. She did not complain about the numerous side effects she experienced. She possessed an inner strength from the moment we were told she had cancer. Her mindset was that all her energy would be spent doing whatever it took to get well. I believe that Rose Ann was prepared to walk through a wall if she had to.

By attending each chemotherapy session with her, I discovered that all the patients looked very sick, but they all seemed to possess a powerful inner strength. These pa-tients had a very positive attitude and as sick as they were, never hesitated to smile and joke. That's called laughing in the face of adversity.

This chemo room was filled with people being courte-ous, polite, thoughtful, kind, patient, and appreciative. They always thanked anyone who helped them. They held in very high regard their nurses and doctors. Every visitor who en-tered the chemo room behaved in the same fashion. The power they demonstrated was phenomenal. Helping Rose Ann, and being a part of this experience was a privilege.

The following conclusions were made:

1. The patients and caretakers had a laser-type focus aimed at defeating cancer
2. All the elements of both an honorable attitude and patience were present
3. Courage, kindness, thoughtfulness, and gratitude were prevalent
4. A **stringing** (of 1 through 3) created a synergy that was so powerful, it became contagious

If stringing just three teacher weapons can have a powerful and synergistic effect upon entering a chemo room, think of the power in stringing all of the teacher weapons in this entire book.

Although cancer is a very powerful disease that kills, the power of the people in the chemo room was nothing short of awesome. By helping my wife, I was rewarded by spending time with some very extraordinary people. These people were fighting for their lives. They did not allow themselves to be troubled by the small things in life.

Instead, they appreciated the little things in life, like a fluffed up pillow behind their heads. They conserved their energy for the important battles. These extraordinary people are true warriors, and Rose Ann is one of them.

TRUE WARRIORS

True warriors focus on forcing an opponent to acquiesce, while blocking out their own pain and discomfort. True warriors don't complain, boast, or put on "Pity parties." Instead they focus on helping others in need, even though they are facing very demanding challenges of their own.

These warriors have a pleasant disposition, and remain cool, calm and collected under the most trying circumstances. I didn't meet these warriors in a dojo, at the mall or even in a place of worship. I met them in a chemo room. Cancer is a very tough opponent, but these true and real-life warriors took the honorable path in the way they fought for their lives.

In all the training and fighting that I did in martial arts, I don't believe that I reached the level of a true warrior. On the other hand, Rose Ann who is the absolute love of my life for over 35 years is not only a true warrior, but my personal hero. She transformed the title of this chapter from "Oh! No! Not the Timer," to "Oh! Yes! the Timer." It's time to transform ourselves into true warriors by facing our challenges with courage.

This chapter recognizes there are many people in all walks of life, including teachers, who are extraordinary people, true warriors, and unsung heroes. So begin to **string** the teacher weapons throughout this book and experience real power.

This chapter is dedicated to Rose Ann and the extraordinary nurses, staff, doctors and patients we met in our journey.

Just a Thought ...

Winners meet life's challenges head on, knowing there are no guarantees, while giving it all they've got.

Chapter 9 - Teacher Weapons Review

WEAPON: AN HONORABLE ATTITUDE

- Don't place blame on others
- Have a positive outlook
- Show respect in the way you talk and act
- Be sincere to yourself and others

WEAPON: PRACTICING PATIENCE

- It's more than just waiting for something to happen; it's having a calm state of mind while you're waiting
- Don't easily give up on yourself or others
- Be tolerant of others and their differences

WEAPON: STRINGING

Integrating at least two teacher weapons together each day in our methods of operation in the classroom is referred to as *stringing*. In this particular chapter, we initially suggested stringing the elements of an honorable attitude with the elements of practicing patience.

The patients in the chemo room were stringing the following in their fight against cancer.

- A laser-type focus
- An honorable attitude
- The elements of patience
- Courage
- Kindness
- Thoughtfulness
- Gratitude

Together these are very powerful weapons.

Chapter 10

Bully for You

"Nothing in life is to be feared,
it is only to be understood."

Marie Curie

Bully, Bully

Bullying is an important issue in our schools that needs special attention. With all the media attention that has been given to the negative effects that student bullying can have, many school districts have rules, procedures and consequences in place that deal with this type of student behavior. Therefore, this focus is not about the student bullies; it is about the **adult bullying** that is taking place.

Bullying behavior can occur at any positional level in a school district. The superintendents of schools, administrators, school board members, teachers, nonprofessional staff members, and irate parents are examples of the individuals who attempt to bully others. They try to manipulate, coerce, and intimidate. If you are of the belief that adult bullying is almost nonexistent in schools, you may change your position after reading this chapter.

The definition of the word "bully" is "1: to treat abusively 2: to affect by means of force or coercion ~ vi: to use browbeating language or behavior: BLUSTER syn intimidate." (*Merriam-Webster's Collegiate Dictionary 11ᵗʰ ed.*, 163)

As a teacher, assistant principal and elementary principal in public schools for over 30 years, I witnessed numerous episodes of adult bullying on teachers and administrators. There were superiors who regularly used their positional power to intimidate others. This was their predominant positional leadership style of choice. Bringing up a concern or asking a question, no matter how intelligent or relevant, could bring forth severe consequences.

In the words they frequently used, "We always have to be team players." Any mistake someone made that created work for them was immediately followed with a browbeating and belittling conference. These positional leaders used any loophole within the boundaries of the law so they could exert their authority to legally bully others. It didn't matter to them how insignificant a mistake was. What really mattered to them was how the mistake negatively affected their image.

These condemning approaches were used by positional leaders who were very legalistically focused. They seldom accepted trial and error as a part of anyone's learning process except their own or someone they favored. They pretended to know it all, and had few skills to do anything they directed others to do. Giving directives was the often-used form of communication.

The educational and working atmosphere this created was stifling, exhausting and left little room for creativity.

These bullies are continually doing a great deal of damage to our schools. They hide their tactics by camouflaging them as necessary in performing their daily duties. Since their job was difficult with a great deal of responsibility, they feel no one should question their techniques. In essence they believe they have a license to bully.

In actuality, they are clueless to what constitutes **real leadership**. According to the Bennis and Nanus Study, the 10 common characteristics of effective leaders are: (Bennis and Nanus 1985, 78-80)

- Clear sense of purpose
- Persistence
- Self-knowledge
- Perpetual learners
- Love of their work
- Ability to attract and energize people
- Mature in human relations
- Risk takers
- Fail-safe
- Ultimately followers

Bullies who are positional leaders do not possess the 10 characteristics of effective leaders, nor do they have any desire to learn real leadership skills and techniques. Please note that I used the term *positional leaders,* because authentic leaders don't regularly resort to coercion. Instead, they use weapons and techniques that promote partnerships with their colleagues and subordinates, rather than using fear to manipulate them.

This reference is not meant for an administrator who is properly reprimanding or taking the necessary legal steps towards the inappropriate behavior of a staff member. Nor is it meant for administrators who correct staff members when they are deliberately or repetitively insubordinate.

Instead, it is directed at administrators who regularly treat their staff as the enemy. They use threats and coercion techniques, rather than collaboration, coaching and counseling techniques. No one has the right to bully others. Is anyone at your school attempting to bully you? I hope not, however, there are teacher weapons available to you if they are. These teacher weapons were developed with the martial art of aikido mindset that no one should be allowed to bully.

No Bullies Allowed

There are bullies who infiltrate every aspect of our lives. From the person on the highway who is tailgating us, to the customer in line at the discount store who is verbally abusing the cashier. It can even be the person who is impatiently waiting in line, while verbally abusing everyone around them.

Bullying is happening all too frequently in our communities and our schools. It is not a rare occurrence to have a bully invade our lives. Bullies have no height, weight or age requirement. Both males and females can partake in this behavior.

It's not hard to be a bully; just be abusive, cruel and take unfair advantage of people. Wouldn't it be great if there was a place where bullies were drained of all their power and immediately were inoculated with humility? There is.

In the martial art of aikido, there are no competitive tournaments because the techniques are too brutal and devastating. When training and in taking promotional tests, there are no weight classes.

In this martial art, it does not matter how big or small one's opponents are. It does not matter how strong or weak one is. Aikido techniques effectively bring the attackers to their knees. Bullying tendencies when training in aikido quickly get corrected. They immediately force one to give up by using a tapping gesture to stop the technique and its pain. This act compels one to use humility.

The major goal in aikido is to transform a foe into a partner. It uses the force of an oncoming attacker against the attacker. The attacker gives up the attack, while they are in a compromisingly-painful position.

Aikido techniques are only used defensively. If there is no attack, there is no aikido to be used. Bullying and aikido are at opposite ends of the spectrum. These experiences helped extrapolate some teacher weapons in dealing with bullies.

SAVE OUR SCHOOLS FROM BULLIES

Bullies can attack us in many ways. They direct attacks at others by using guilt and associate it with any possible fault they can find in others. These bullies used threats, chastising comments, and possible punishments into forcing people to follow what they want them to do.

However, this becomes totally unacceptable when their directives are illegal. In the process of fighting off these unsuccessful bullying attacks, our energy gets drained while they continue in their attempt to break our teaching spirit.

The teacher weapon that has successfully countered these attacks is adhering to the motto, "*No one will ever infect me with condemnation and guilt. They will not break my teaching spirit.*" In addition, by admitting one's idiosyncrasies and defining where improvement is needed, one can make incremental improvements that will eventually lead to a major breakthrough.

This entire process takes perseverance and endurance. Making excuses or blaming others is unacceptable. This teacher weapon is *using conviction towards self improvement.* It allows us to stop competing and comparing, and focus on what's really important. This is **true** power, because it helps us to work towards our full potential.

On the other side of the spectrum is what the bullies use as their major weapon, condemnation. This has *artificial* power, because it promotes self-torment and paralysis.

For example, if administrators are bullies and use condemnation, they create fear and anxiousness throughout the school district. Teachers and staff become afraid to say anything negative, while their inner thoughts become increasingly negative. Self-survival becomes their predominant mode. Trusting anyone becomes a rare occurrence for fear that a slip of the tongue could get back to the administrator.

Bullying and condemnation creates a great deal of isolation. This is leadership at its worst, because foreboding becomes engrained into the school's atmosphere. Foreboding means being ready to anticipate that bad things are going to continually happen. Living as a teacher and a principal in these environments led me to the next teacher weapon for fighting bullies: *use your pain to help others gain.*

When feeling depleted, down, and having one's teaching spirit constantly under attack, a change is needed. This change can be possible by doing random acts of kindness throughout the school day to colleagues, staff and students.

Within a short period of time, a renewed teaching spirit will be activated, and along with it, a feeling of empowerment. It will now be possible to come to school in a pleasing disposition. This can be contagious and begin to positively affect others. This is the very first step in using your personal power to find true power.

True power is not found externally—it is what you will experience internally. When an administrator only relies on positional power, no real leadership is exhibited. Therefore, it can start at the teachers' level.

In other words, real leadership is earned, while positional leadership is appointed. Real leadership contains personal power. It would be an optimum situation, if the positional leader also used personal power.

Administrators who are real leaders know their success depends on the success of those they supervise. They should frequently ask those they supervise; "How can I help you succeed?"

There are far too many school districts that accept bullying as a common leadership style. They resort to command, control and comply. They need to recognize they are taking part in sabotaging their own schools. This myopic view must be corrected, because this is one of the most damaging factors that exist in our schools today. It is routinely being camouflaged by positional leaders.

Administrators need to achieve real collaboration with the teachers and the staff in our schools. It can have a positive and multiplicative effect in real teaching. We need to eradicate a pervasive "Good ole boy" approach that promotes bullying and subtracts from the real teaching realm.

Too much emphasis is being placed on the textbooks, educational programs, the most up-to-date computer software, and tests. Although these are legitimate areas of interest, they don't approach the importance of real educational leadership and the promotion of a powerful teaching spirit. Our schools can't afford to waste any more time, energy, services and teachable moments, because of the chasm that exists between our positional educational leaders and leaders with personal power.

Real educational leadership is not just how one performs, but how we perform together. Use your teacher weapons and start responding to the antiquated bullying attacks. Remember these attacks are made in lieu of the real leadership skills that need to be utilized.

Take the first step in the path to success by confronting bullies and promoting real leadership by using your personal power. Administrators need to have an attitude of service instead of trying to command, control and force people to comply.

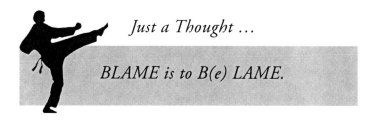

Just a Thought ...

BLAME is to B(e) LAME.

Chapter 10 - Teacher Weapons Review

WEAPON: SECURE LEGAL COUNSEL FROM AN ATTORNEY, EITHER PRIVATELY OR THROUGH YOUR UNION, IF NECESSARY

WEAPON: USE THE MOTTO, "NO ONE WILL EVER INFECT ME WITH CONDEMNATION AND GUILT. THEY WILL NOT BREAK MY TEACHING SPIRIT."

WEAPON: USING CONVICTION TOWARDS SELF-IMPROVEMENT

- Embrace self evaluation by admitting idiosyncrasies
- Define where improvement is needed
- Make regular small incremental improvements that will eventually lead us to a major breakthrough
- Perform self evaluation regularly
- This entire process takes perseverance and endurance
- Don't make excuses or blame others
- This is true power, because it helps us to work towards our full potential
- Abandon command, control and forced compliance and replace it with a service heart

WEAPON: USE YOUR PAIN TO HELP OTHERS GAIN

- Smile while doing random acts of kindness to colleagues, staff and students each day, which will help renew your teaching spirit
- Don't be infected by a toxic atmosphere—instead affect others in a positive way

Chapter 11

Be an Energizer Buddy

"The energy of the mind is the essence of life."
Aristotle

It's Test Time …
How Could I Have Prepared for This?

A promotional test in martial arts is given periodically to students who reach certain benchmarks. At each specified level, the students must complete the necessary hours of training, know the attacks and the defensive techniques along with the corresponding Japanese terminology.

Each testing student is responsible for the current testing techniques, as well as the techniques in all of their previous tests. When I took a promotional test in aikido, it turned out to be a life-changing experience.

Being well-prepared to take my second promotional test in aikido, meant all the techniques and their Japanese terms were learned. Being in top physical condition was also a must. However, I was not ready for what was about to happen.

It was test time on a Saturday. The *dojo* was at full capacity. It was announced that three different aikido schools were being tested together. I was paired up with an unfamiliar student from a different school. From the start of the test, this student applied his defensive techniques so hard, it gave me over-the-top pain.

Aikido techniques are supposed to inflict some pain to the attacker; however, when giving the appropriate signal, which is a tapping on our uniform (*gi*) or the mat, the defender is suppose to ease up on his torque. Communication between the attacker and the defender is of utmost importance, since we are considered partners. Training is hard, but should be done safely. My partner did not heed to any of my easing up signals, and I was paying dearly for it.

Testing with an Energy Zapper

After having trained and tested with all kinds of injuries and even some broken bones, I never experienced pain this intense. The concentration of my partner was solely on his individual techniques—he was oblivious and uncaring about anything else. This was taking its toll on my mind, body and spirit. Having only completed one-third of the techniques that were on this test, my completion was in serious doubt.

My first thought was to put this guy in the hospital. However, this action is considered dishonorable and unacceptable. In the meantime, the continuous pain was stealing every ounce of my energy. This testing partner was an energy zapper. The conditioning level that took me months to reach was being negated, and hyperventilation was beginning. Throwing in the towel now seemed plausible.

TESTING WITH MY ENERGIZER BUDDY

At my darkest moment, something positive and powerful started to take place. Jim, who is an advanced student in our *dojo*, noticed my struggle. He positioned himself close to where I was testing.

Although no talking is permitted during a promotional test, each time we were in Jim's vicinity, he whispered words of encouragement. For example, "Paul stay strong; you can do this. Slow down your breathing. He can't hurt you any more than he already has. You're doing it and you can finish."

By giving these words of encouragement, it triggered in me a similar internal dialogue. Jim was my energizer buddy who helped me start to energize. Now my thoughts were, "My partner has been using all the possible power that he could muster up, so he can't hurt me any more.

Although he somewhat knows the techniques, his skills are not all that great, which is why he is resorting to putting so much force into them. Don't focus on the pain. Slow down your breathing even more and quickly start to recover."

This internal dialogue was continued throughout the remainder of the test. The depleted energy level that once felt amazingly drained was replenished. The former unbearable pain now seemed insignificant. The energy zapper seemed powerless despite using the same amount of torque.

THE DISCOVERY OF REAL POWER

After completing and passing this promotional test, I thanked Jim, my energizer buddy. He commented that testing with my assigned partner was an accomplishment that he will never forget.

On this particular promotional test day, I discovered real power. It was **not** in learning the Japanese terminology. It was **not** in knowing the offensive and defensive aikido techniques. It was **not** in attaining a high level of physical conditioning. It was **not** in being thoroughly prepared to perform the techniques that were in my previous promotional test.

The positive internal dialogue that was triggered by my energizer buddy is where I found my real power. I am thankful for the help that Jim gave me that day. He interrupted my trip on the road to disempowerment and helplessness, by helping me discover the energizer buddy that is inside all of us. The benefits from the energizer buddy were immediate, powerful and life changing. Do you think these benefits are only applicable to taking martial arts promotional tests? No way!

THE NEED FOR THE TEACHER'S ENERGIZER BUDDY SYSTEM

This experience helped me discover a very powerful teacher weapon called the *teacher's energizer buddy system*. This weapon was useful time and time again. It is especially helpful when encountering very difficult situations that elicit a great deal of pain.

In the teaching profession, your partners, who are inflicting you with pain, are not the disconnected aikido students. Your difficult partners could include: students, parents, colleagues, administrators, non-professional staff, and state or federal education bureaucrats.

Other difficult partners can be in the form of a new testing program, or a newly adopted district textbook that was imposed on everyone. These difficult partners can sabotage our efforts, and make a simple situation seem next to impossible. They can also be a major source in depleting a teacher's energy.

FORMING THE TEACHER'S ENERGIZER BUDDY SYSTEM

My first *teacher's energizer buddy system* experience started my second year as a high school teacher. Our department was so large; it was split up into teaching teams. My assigned team had weekly meetings after school. The discussions included: teaching methodology, subject matter, testing, and dealing with the difficult students in our classrooms.

This team had a great mix of teachers that included the wise veteran teachers and the full-of-energy new teachers. This team experienced many successes. Our students collectively performed exemplary on the state tests. Some of our most talented students won academic awards in statewide competitions and for four straight years took top honors.

This produced a great deal of positive publicity for our high school and our team. Many teachers in our high school wondered why our team had so much success. They visited our classes and had frank discussions with us.

It was obvious that the teachers and students were **real** partners in these classrooms. They fed off each others' positive energy, worked hard and wasted little class time. Overall, the learning process was harmonious and fun. Eventually, this team disbanded when some of its members became administrators and others retired. This was the beginning of the formation of the *teacher's energizer buddy system* concept.

VALIDATION TO THE ENERGIZER BUDDY SYSTEM

In my educational career, I worked in a high school and two different elementary schools. This does not include adjunct teaching at a community college and a four-year college. The experiences in each school incrementally added to the ongoing evolvement of the energizer buddy system.

By becoming more and more astute in noticing who the energizer buddies were, and what weapons they utilized, it was easy to notice the differences in the teachers who were **not** energizer buddies. This led to the discovery of the two dimensions to the *teacher's energizer buddy system.*

The first includes the powerful and positive forces in *energizer-buddy posturing.* The second dimension is identifying the negative forces in *pejorative posturing.* This second dimension is equally important, because we need to quickly identify when we enter this dimension, so that we can quickly transition out of it.

In my last twelve years in education, I had the ultimate privilege of working in an elementary school in which the principal and over 95% of the teachers and staff regularly were part of an *energizer buddy system.* When people entered this school, they would often state, "There is a wonderful feeling that one gets coming in here."

This was a school where hard work, high standards, and fun were the norm. This elementary school received many awards in recognition of their accomplishments. These included the excellent state testing results of the students in all the state-designated categories. It also was recognized as a very peaceful school and won the state's "Peaceful School Award." This award was personally presented to the school by the Lieutenant Governor of New York State.

Everyone who worked in this school had a student-centered focus. There was a pervasive attitude that everyone had to do their very best each day to help our students. There were no acceptable excuses for mediocrity in attitude, effort and happiness. The parents appreciated the education their children were receiving, and they embraced the school's atmosphere.

Were there problems and challenges? Absolutely, but every problem becomes possible to solve with so many energizer buddies. I was so fortunate to be the energizer buddy principal of this school for twelve years. What an honor it was to work with such an energizing group of people. You see, being an energizer buddy can be very contagious.

TWO DIMENSIONS OF THE ENERGIZER BUDDY SYSTEM
ENERGIZER BUDDY POSTURING DIMENSION

This dimension is much more than just helping or being helped in a crisis situation. It is regularly using real collaboration with the principal, staff and students to strive to be the best that we can be. It is striving to have an exemplary school, environment and atmosphere.

In this dimension, a teacher energizer buddy is a person who can help change a negative situation into a positive one. Energizer buddies are skillful educators who go *above and beyond the call of duty* regularly and gladly in helping others.

When more than one energizer buddy works together, the synergy can be quite astounding. The teachers lounge can be an aid or a problem to the energizer buddies. Negative talk must be replaced by focusing on the positives that exist in the school. Energizer buddies regularly exhibit many of the following traits. So examine this list and strive to acquire as many of these traits as possible.

TRAITS FOR ENERGIZER BUDDY POSTURING

1. High performance with integrity
2. Encouraging with your thoughts and words
3. High energy and very creative
4. Kind and merciful
5. Unselfish – givers, not takers
6. Patient and hopeful (reluctance to never give up)
7. Positive attitude and upbeat
8. Enthusiastic
9. Steadfast and dependable
10. Dedicated and highly committed to school, profession, and students
11. Great sense of humor and is fun to be around
12. Retrievers who rarely point (refer to chapter 3)
13. Hard workers with a great deal of endurance
14. Intrinsically motivated
15. Eternal optimists—nothing is impossible; can change negative situations into positive
16. Appreciative and grateful
17. Mainly focused on arriving at solutions to problems
18. Genuinely happy
19. Collaborative in solving many problems

20. Focused on working to improve professional skills
21. Focused on personal improvement
22. Consistently working towards building and keeping positive momentum
23. Ability to turn an aversive situation or challenge into a success
24. Showing leadership through actions and success
25. Well-respected and possesses a great deal of integrity
26. Seldom complaining because personal comfort zone is secondary
27. External conditions don't dictate happiness
28. Very seldom uses excuses
29. Consistently goes above and beyond the call of duty
30. Ability to admit mistakes
31. Actions promote synergy
32. Celebrates accomplishments
33. Able to view themselves as victors
34. Responsive to situations, while being slow to react

The more traits that are used in your energizer buddy posture, the more **real or personal** power you will have. This will have a greater impact in changing positive situations to even better ones. It will also have a greater impact in changing a negative situation into a positive one.

There are varying degrees to the power that energizer buddy posturing can help you attain. The degree of power is directly related to how many there are and how often you exhibit these traits. Teacher energizer buddies who possess and consistently perform these traits are great teachers and **real** leaders in their schools. They may not be formally recognized as such, but the proof becomes obvious in how they are universally respected, appreciated and admired.

What percentage of the teachers, staff and administration at your school are energizer buddies? There is no time like the present to make things better. Make a commitment today to work at being a powerful energizer buddy in your school.

Remember it can be very contagious. So let's start positively affecting ourselves and others in striving to develop a critical mass of energizer buddies that create a positive culture.

PEJORATIVE POSTURING DIMENSION

This *pejorative posturing dimension* in the energizer buddy system is a very negative and counterproductive one. You need to be able to identify when you enter this dimension so that you can very quickly transition out of it.

When you enter this dimension, you are in a very negative state of mind and believe that only bad things are possible. Overreaction to your negative thoughts, words, and disposition can be dominating. Solving even the simplest of problems becomes a monumental task.

In this dimension, you are not positively affecting others; instead, you are negatively infecting others. You are seldom happy and have a mile-long list of what needs to happen for you to be happy.

In essence, you are controlled by your circumstances. You have acquired the **useless** skill of making a good situation bad or a bad situation worse. This can be consciously or unconsciously done. We all have times when we enter this dimension.

Teachers experience just about every pejorative posturing trait at some time during their career. The more pejorative traits you possess, the more disempowered and ineffective you will be. So examine the following 20 traits and use this list to help you stay out of this dimension.

Pejorative Posturing Traits

1. Reacts to situations, but slow to respond
2. Consumed with doubt and fear
3. Does not distinguish between small problems or large problems
4. Mainly concerned about being out of our comfort zone and not doing hard work
5. Keeps the negative as the focal point
6. Belittles and discredits others
7. Complains and whines
8. Has a long list of personal rules that must be followed to be happy
9. Is seldom happy and not fun to be around
10. Is highly critical
11. Is self-centered
12. Is selfish
13. Regards any change as an inconvenience
14. Has negative attitude towards change
15. At times, runs away from work
16. Is very excuse-oriented
17. Regards everything as a potential problem
18. Chooses dictatorship as the favorite choice of operation
19. Spends too much time and energy thinking of strife
20. Views themselves as victims

Please keep in mind, there is one thing about pejorative posturing that is similar to the energizer buddy posture; it can be contagious. Since this posturing is not a good thing, be very alert to its presence.

When entering this dimension, there is a tendency to have dominant thoughts of fear, doubt and panic. The key is to possess as few of these 20 traits as possible.

Having experienced both of these dimensions, it becomes very evident which one makes for a better attitude and life. Being in an energizer buddy posture can be very empowering and rewarding, while being in a pejorative posture leaves one disempowered and overwhelmed.

Begin to be a positive and powerful energizer buddy to yourself and others. Remember it, too, can be very contagious.

Just a Thought ...

*Positivism and negativism
are contagious.*

Chapter 11 - Teacher Weapons Review

WEAPON: DISCOVER YOUR REAL POWER

- Be your own energizer buddy and discover real and personal power by making your internal dialogue positive
- Real and personal power can have a great impact in changing a negative situation into a positive one
- Real and personal power can also have a great impact in changing a positive situation into an even better one

WEAPON: USE THE TWO DIMENSIONS OF THE ENERGIZER BUDDY SYSTEM

ENERGIZER BUDDY POSTURING DIMENSION

- This dimension lists 34 traits contained in this chapter
- The more traits that you exhibit, the more real power you will acquire
- Teacher energizer buddies who possess and consistently exhibit these traits are great teachers and real leaders in their schools
- These traits can be contagious and positively affect others

PEJORATIVE POSTURING DIMENSION

- This dimension lists 20 traits contained in this chapter
- If you enter this dimension, you need to make a quick exit
- In this dimension, you have a very negative state of mind
- You believe that only bad things are possible
- The more of these traits that you exhibit at one time, the more you feel disempowered and ineffective

- You utilize the useless skill of making a good situation bad, or a bad situation worse
- These traits can also be contagious and can negatively infect others

Chapter 12

Food for Thought

"Learning without thinking is useless. Thinking without learning is dangerous."

Confucius
(The Analects)

Starting Your Day

Before a martial arts class starts, the students line up on the *tatami* mats in a kneeling position, and meditate. While they are controlling their breathing, they're slowing down their heart rate, and clearing their minds.

Everyone is striving to start each class with a renewed and fresh mindset. This preparation makes them ready and alert. It is a necessary step, to help ensure their safety.

START EVERY DAY WITH A RENEWED AND FRESH MINDSET

Being able to start every day in school with a renewed and a fresh mindset can also be a very powerful teacher weapon. By developing and using the following four steps, you can prepare to have a renewed and fresh mindset each day.

1. Take a Daily Thoughts Inventory

Each day, take an inventory of your thoughts. Don't make today dependent on what happened yesterday. Don't make today dependent on what happened at home this morning. Don't make today dependent on what happened on the way to work.

Realize the power that is contained in your present thoughts. Purposely pay attention to what you are thinking. This will allow you to control your thoughts and not have your thoughts control you.

2. Use Empowering Words to Help You Control Your Thoughts

You can be successful at controlling your thoughts by using empowering words. These words can act as modifiers for your problems and intensifiers for your efforts.

For example, I had a student in my class who continued to be disruptive despite all the meetings with his parent, guidance counselor, principal, social worker and school psychologist. He was placed in the internal suspension program and was even externally suspended from school. Although his behavior did improve somewhat, he was still generally disruptive.

In my discussions concerning this student, I was careful to **never** state that he was my most difficult student. I chose to use modifying words like, "This student was **a bit of a challenge** today in class." By speaking this way, it was clear that I was not giving up on this student and was able to persevere with a healthy attitude.

At the same time, whenever this student showed improvements in his behavior or effort, a positive intensifier was used in the form of a compliment. An example of this is, "You **really worked hard** in class today; see you tomorrow."

By consciously using word modifiers and intensifiers, it paved the way for this student to do his very best. At the end of the third quarter, during teacher conference day, this student earned a grade of 83% and reached a satisfactory level in his behavior.

In a discussion at his parent conference, his father divulged that my class was his favorite. It took the better half of a school year to achieve this breakthrough. Using modifiers and intensifiers enabled me to persevere and experience success with this student.

By using empowering words in both your external and internal dialogue, it will enable you to experience a great deal of success. By regularly referring to the following quote, it will help to ensure your belief in the power in words. "Without knowing the force of words, it is impossible to know men." (Confucius [Analects])

3. FILTER THE IMPORTANT THOUGHTS FROM THE NONSENSE

By taking a daily inventory of your thoughts, you can filter important thoughts from the nonsense. This filtering allows you to get the clutter out of your mind. It will help you to realize how many made-up rules you need to follow.

By examining each rule, you will realize that many of them are down-right foolish. You will also see the needless stress and frustration that emanates from these nonsensical rules. Keeping track and following many of these rules is exhausting and can steal your energy and happiness.

4. EDIT YOUR PERSONAL AND PROFESSIONAL RULES

By being honest and writing down all of your made-up rules, you will become aware that many of them are outright ridiculous. Believing these rules have to be followed each day for you to be a satisfied and successful teacher is self-deceit. Although you may be a very successful teacher, these rules are setting you up to be very unhappy.

Every one of these rules needs a close examination. Some need to be discarded, while others need to be modified. For example, all the students in my classes were required to have their homework assignments completed and handed in each day. This was a steadfast and necessary rule.

However, my personal rule needed to be changed on how I reacted when students didn't have their assignments. Previously, I would get very upset and lecture on how important these assignments were. This rule was modified to remove my being upset by requiring the students to hand in the missed assignment along with the next day's assignment.

If this was not done, their parent would be personally contacted. If they weren't available at work, they were contacted at home. On some occasions, this would require a personal visit to their home. This procedure only had to be followed for about three weeks, before it became clear that I wasn't bluffing.

Did it work? You bet. These students may have been in arrears with their assignments in other classes, but not mine. This procedure allowed me to be a dedicated and concerned teacher, without being emotionally drained.

A similar approach was taken when students received failing grades. Again, instead of lecturing the students, they were encouraged to attend extra classes during their study hall and/or come for help before or after school. If a student didn't take any of these steps, a personal contact to their parents was made.

The students responded really well, because my request to the parents was to ground them until they were notified when their child regained a passing grade. It is amazing how hard-working these students became, and how quickly they improved their grades. For some reason, high school students don't like any of their weekend plans curtailed. This made the teaching and learning process a great deal easier.

On a personal note, whenever I had a conflict or argument with a relative or friend, I examined my rules to see if there was a ridiculous rule in the middle of it all. Instantaneously, some ridiculous rules were uncovered.

Instead of continuing the argument, the infecting rule was deleted and my point of view changed. Deleting or changing ridiculous rules led me to the path in clearer thinking. It didn't take long to discover, the less rules, the better off one is.

Make it a priority to take time regularly and examine all of your rules. Although deleting and changing rules can be a painful process initially, it is a necessary experience. Consider this process to be the necessary growing pains to achieve a more enjoyable and rewarding experience. I have never regretted the day that I started this process; it has become a life-long one for me.

ANOTHER CONFRONTATION

Although the day may be started with a renewed and fresh mindset, it won't take long before encountering conflicts and confrontations. These situations can be viewed similar to how one safely trains in martial arts.

There are no acceptable excuses to act irresponsibly when training in a *dojo*. It can cause someone to get injured.

When making an honest mistake, it is immediately followed by an apology and a proper bow. An honest mistake is an error that is made by one with the honorable intention of not hurting others. This is the underlying concept to be used in dealing with conflicts and confrontations.

As a teenager, one might say, "Those who run away may live to fight another day." Keeping in mind this saying, there are instances when an immediate confrontation may not be the best course of action. In other words, there are times when it may be better to flee rather than fight.

For instance, this may be true if the incident is a minor one or is a one-time incident. No one is perfect and there may be little gained in having a confrontation. This is especially true, if it involves an honest mistake. However, when a confrontation is necessary or inevitable, keep these five steps in mind:

1. Pick the time for the confrontation wisely. Timing is very important. For example, after having a very busy week, and just before leaving on Friday, may not be a good choice.

2. Start the conversation with a positive value statement. For example, "I value your hard work and all the effort that you give, how can we ..."

3. Bring up any of the mistakes you previously made as an example to show that perfection is not expected and that you are not being unreasonable. Everyone makes mistakes; however, repeatedly making the same one is a problem. The definition of insanity is doing the same thing over and over, while expecting different results.
4. Stay away from endless lecturing. Talk about specific events and facts. Refrain from giving opinions or being judgmental.
5. Be honest and compassionate.

These five steps can help you be successful in your confrontations and throughout your professional life.

THE DUMP AND RUN

Because of the serious nature of martial arts, many boundaries are placed when executing the offensive and defensive techniques. This was helpful in dealing with what my wife calls *the dump and run.*

This occurs when you have a conversation with a person who predominately talks about their problems. This person believes their problems and circumstances are the most severe in the entire world. Their verbal marathon consists of piggy-backing all their problems together to convince anyone and everyone how terrible their circumstances are.

In their mind no one has experienced what they are going through. They constantly have a black cloud over their head and dim the lighting every time they enter a room. They relive these circumstances over and over again to anyone who will listen to them.

The person who is telling (*dumps*) their stories, feels better temporarily and then leaves (*runs*). On the other hand, the person who is dumped on is emotionally depleted. Most people know someone who uses *the dump and run*.

FENDING OFF THE DUMP AND RUN

Predominately, people who regularly use *the dump and run* ignore any suggestions or solutions that are offered. Their only goal is to "relieve" themselves on others. In martial arts, boundaries are placed on techniques; this is the same concept used in fending off *the dump and run*.

1. Purposely limit the amount of time that you talk to them, whether it is on the phone or in person.
2. Interject into the conversation a question of what kind of help have they searched for? If they ignore the question, interrupt them and conclude the conversation by telling them that it seems they need to get more help with these difficult problems. Wish them well and leave.

By taking just these few steps in designing boundaries to your conversation, you will limit their toxic conversation which drains your energy and takes away your balance. Limit anyone and everyone who tries to use *the dump and run* on you.

Just a Thought ...

Edit your personal and professional rules, and be led to a path of clear thinking.

Chapter 12 - Teacher Weapons Review

WEAPON: TO START EVERY DAY WITH A RENEWED AND FRESH MINDSET, FOLLOW THE FOUR STEPS

1. Take a daily thoughts inventory
2. Use empowering words to help you control your thoughts

   Use modifiers for your problems

   Use intensifiers for your efforts
3. Filter important thoughts from the nonsense
4. Edit personal and professional rules

   Delete or change ridiculous rules

   Follow these rules to a path of clear thinking

WEAPON: WHEN A CONFRONTATION IS NECESSARY, FOLLOW THE FIVE STEPS

1. Pick the time for the confrontation wisely
2. Start the conversation with a positive value statement
3. Bring up any mistake you made previously to show you are not expecting perfection
4. Talk about specific events and facts
5. Be honest and compassionate

WEAPON: FENDING OFF THE DUMP AND RUN

The dump and run occurs when a person believes their problems are the most severe in the entire world

They dump their stories on others, to help them feel relief, while leaving the person they dumped on feeling emotionally depleted

Two steps in fending off *the dump and run:*

1. Purposely limit the amount of time talking to them whether on the phone or in person
2. Interject in the conversation a question regarding what kind of help they have sought and put a limit on their dumping time

Chapter 13

You Know What I Mean?

"The aim of an argument or discussion should not be victory but understanding."

Anonymous

A State of Mind

In martial arts, to execute an attack or a defensive technique, one must be in a calm and assertive state. A calm state is when your emotions are being controlled, and they are not controlling you. An assertive state is being ready and willing to effectively deal with what is about to happen.

When in a calm and assertive state, a martial artist is able to smile in the face of adversity because negative thoughts and body tension are absent. Imagine how valuable being in this state could be for a classroom teacher each day. By consistently striving to be calm and assertive, you will discover the real power in this teacher weapon.

THREE STEPS IN PREPARING TO BE CALM AND ASSERTIVE

1. Daily preparation is required to be calm and assertive. It starts by attending to your **physical state**. This includes attaining a determined focus, maintaining good posture

and using the proper breathing techniques. Give special attention not to clench your hands or tense your jaw, because body tension is your enemy.

2. Once your physical state is achieved, use the following thoughts to help you attain balance and calmness. The first thought is, "Nothing is as bad as it seems, and nothing is as good as it seems. It's somewhere in the middle." The second thought is, "Don't take life too seriously, because you're never going to get out of it alive." By repetitively thinking these thoughts, you can maintain a healthy perspective.

3. Once you achieve calmness in your thoughts, you can now concentrate on assertiveness. Communication is a critical component that will determine how powerful and effective you will be.

COMMUNICATION AND YOUR LEARNING STYLE PREFERENCES

A vast majority of teachers think they are excellent communicators. However, teachers are the first ones to admit there are far too many instances when their listeners just don't get the message. True communication brings about shared understanding.

I learned in my first course in education that each of us had a preferred way in how we learn. About 30% learn visually (seeing), 25% learn auditorily (hearing), and 45% learn kinesthetically (doing).

Visual learners use pictures. When using this learning style, people talk fast, because they are trying to catch up to their mental pictures or movie. While engaging in conversation these learners may prefer to say things like, "I see where you're coming from."

Others prefer learning by paying very close attention to what they hear. They scrutinize every word that is said, and talk at a slower rate. They are tuned into the CD that is re-playing in their mind. They may prefer to say, "I hear what you are saying."

Still others learn by doing. They prefer to use their bodily-kinesthetic learning style or intelligence. According to Armstrong, this intelligence is the ability to use one's body to express ideas and feelings. Some examples of a well-developed bodily-kinesthetic intelligence might be found looking at actors, dancers, athletes, sculptors, mechanics or surgeons."(Armstrong 1994, 7, 30)

People using this learning style may say, "Yeah, I agree with you because that feels about right." When you are communicating with a person using this learning style, don't pass up the opportunity to shake their hand. This is a very small gesture that can be exceptionally helpful in making a connection.

No one learning style preference is better than another, and has nothing to do with one's level of intelligence. You may use all three major ways to learn, but you definitely will have your preference.

The importance of knowing a person's learning preference enables one to make a transition from communicating to connecting. Connecting with people is a much higher standard that allows for shared understanding.

Upgrade from Communicating to Connecting

In the martial arts of aikido, although an attacker has the intent to hurt us, he is still viewed as a partner. Certain defensive techniques are used to convince the attacker that attacking anyone is a very bad decision.

A painful hold or the twisting of an appendage is used until the attacker acquiesces. This acquiescence is what transforms an attacker into a partner. Transferring this from the *dojo* to the classroom creates a climate where everyone is a potential partner. It doesn't matter whether it's an upset parent, student or an administrator.

TEACHER WEAPONS TO USE IN HELPING TO CONNECT

1. Speak in Simple Terms
   Use vocabulary that is easily understood by all.
2. State Your Honorable Intention
   Encourage the parties to disclose their honorable intentions.
3. Agree to Disagree
   Everyone does not have to agree.
4. Be Respectful When Speaking and Listening
   When speaking and listening, it is important to do so in a respectful way, even if you think your partner doesn't deserve it.
5. Smile and mean it
   Make smiling your normal facial expression. It is amazing at the courage that it gives, while enabling potential partners to lessen their body tension. Whether facing a possible confrontation or hearing something positive, smiling is a great demeanor to have and a great weapon to use.
6. Use the knowledge of preferential learning styles to connect with others
   This can become a very powerful teacher weapon. It will enable one to connect with people, where others have failed. By first identifying the learning style of your potential part-

ner, you can specifically tune in to their talking speed and be ready to use specific key words.

For example, people who talk at a fast rate may be visual learners. Target your speaking to them as such. Your reply to them may include, "I see what you mean." When asking a question you may say, "Do you see what I mean?" In your explanations, you may use, "Picture this situation." If you initially use their same speed of talking, you can gradually reduce it to a slower rate and still stay connected.

You can follow the same procedure for auditory and kinesthetic preferential learners, by using the corresponding rate of speech and their preferred descriptors. I first used this weapon at a parent-teacher conference with a father whose daughter was failing.

He entered my classroom in a very angry state. By immediately focusing on the pace of his speech and his words, it was easy to ascertain that his preferential learning style was auditory. By slowing down my rate of speech and being very careful on the words that I used, it created a speed bump that allowed the parent to lose some of his anger.

By using the key phrase, "I hear everything that you just told me," he was able to accept my thoughts on how his daughter could achieve a passing grade. We connected in a big way. His major focus was where it needed to be. A periodic contact system was set up with the parent to keep him up-to-date on his daughter's future performance. Because his learning preference was auditory, he was kept informed by telephone, rather than just sending him a note.

7. Be honest and stay with the facts throughout your communication

By consistently being factual and honest, you will soon earn an honorable reputation as being a fair person. This will make it much easier to connect with your potential partners.

8. Use the power that exists in questions to help you connect

"No question is a stupid one." This is a statement that you may have used in class to encourage your students to ask questions. A student may get high praise from you, when they ask a thoughtful question.

This also applies when you attempt to connect with a potential partner. In other words, quality questions with the right timing can catapult you in establishing a very quick connection.

There are two instances where questions can act as conversational momentum stoppers. Both these instances involve questioning techniques. They are the rapid fire questioning technique and those who ask superficial questions at an inappropriate time. These can cause a disconnection with your potential partners.

The **rapid fire questioning technique** is when one person constantly interrupts the conversation with a series of questions; before one is given time to answer a question. These questions are asked impulsively.

This technique interrupts the positive momentum of the conversation, and brings it to a screeching halt. When this technique is used on you, interrupt in a respectful way.

This can be done by stating that you will answer these questions one at a time. This will transform rapid firing into single question firing, which provides a good opportunity to connect.

The **timing in asking superficial questions** is another technique that can greatly inhibit the positive momentum of a conversation. The user of this technique is impulsively asking a superficial question that is insignificant in nature. However by answering this question immediately, it will steal the positive conversational momentum.

For example, I started to say, "I was really concerned that Bill was severely limping with his bad ..." when I was interrupted with, "Did you see the color of his shirt?" Ignoring this question, I continued, "I was really concerned that Bill was limping severely and hope his bad back wasn't acting up." Remember, Bill had a serious operation just a few months ago, maybe he could use some help."

Superficial questions not only can be momentum stoppers, they can actually give the perception that you don't care. Try not to interrupt conversations with impulsive questions. This can really prevent a meaningful connection.

By connecting with people, we are making them partners in education. Connecting is not a frill any more; it is a must. I have used it for many years, and formed many partnerships. I hope that you can experience this same success.

In summary, by investing your time and effort in being calm and assertive, extraordinary power can be experienced in teaching.

Just a Thought ...

Great communicators always strive to connect and achieve a shared understanding.

Chapter 13 - Teacher Weapons Review

WEAPON: USE THREE STEPS TO PREPARE TO BE CALM AND ASSERTIVE

1. Have a determined focus, good posture and proper breathing

2. Attain balance and calmness by using the following:
   "Nothing is as bad as it seems and nothing is as good as it seems."
   "Don't take life too seriously, because you're never going to get out of it alive."

3. Be assertive through your communication

WEAPON: COMMUNICATION AND THREE LEARNING STYLES

Visual learners use mental pictures and talk fast
Auditory learners scrutinize every word that is said and talk at a slower rate
Kinesthetic learners learn by doing

WEAPON: EIGHT TEACHER WEAPONS TO HELP UPGRADE FROM COMMUNICATING TO CONNECTING

1. Speak in simple terms
2. State your honorable intention
3. Agree to disagree
4. Be respectful when speaking and listening
5. Smile and mean it
6. Use the knowledge of preferential learning styles to connect with others
7. Be honest and stay with the facts throughout your communication

8. Use the power that exists in questions to help connect

Be on the alert for people who use the rapid fire questioning technique and ask superficial questions at an inappropriate time

Chapter 14

Teach Don't Preach

"Perceiving a victory that does not surpass what the masses could know is not the pinnacle of excellence."

Sun Tzu
(The Art of War)

Head and Shoulders above the Rest

When attending many martial arts classes and seminars, I came to realize there were many instructors who were very good, and others were excellent. They were very talented and skillful in their art.

However, there were a few instructors who were *head and shoulders above the rest*. They made a lasting impression, which created a powerful connection with their audience.

These instructors were able to apply the skills they attained in martial arts to their every day lives. They saw martial arts as more than a plethora of techniques. These individuals were humble and possessed an incredible ability to maintain an open mind, which deepened and expanded their knowledge base. This level of vision and wisdom is achieved by only a few.

Please note that many may think they are open-minded, however they fail to acknowledge their own prejudices and idiosyncrasies. Not having true humility is a major stumbling block that can keep us from being open-minded.

EXPANDING YOUR REFERENCES ON PURPOSE

There are a few martial arts instructors, who continuously work on expanding their references. To them, it is a life-long journey in pursuit of their horizon. This horizon is the attainment of wisdom and their references are the sources that keep supplying them knowledge. They have a mindset to utilize their life experiences, which enables them to be better martial artists and, more importantly, better people.

There are many other sources that can help you expand your references as a teacher, in addition to the conventional ones. Some additional sources are books, movies, television, observing people, listening to a song, or going to a place of worship.

You are never on vacation from studying your ever-expanding references. As a matter of fact, you may find some excellent references in the most unlikely places. Therefore, by not placing limitations on where you get your references, you can acquire an ever-growing supply of them.

START YOUR JOURNEY TO YOUR HORIZON

As a teacher, your references are expanded in graduate and postgraduate school. References can additionally be expanded in reading topics such as: self improvement, inspiration, biographies, autobiographies, philosophy, poetry and history.

However, discovering new sources to expand your references can open up a whole new world for you. For instance, after viewing a movie or television show, start to keep notes on quotations or clever comments that are made. It is both fun and useful. If you hear a song that is inspirational, retrieve the lyrics. Following the lyrics while listening to the song can be a very valuable exercise and experience.

With a mindset of pursuing wisdom by expanding your references, your professional reference sources will suddenly increase dramatically. Your over-reliance on the traditional college courses, seminars, in-services, and professional publications will decrease.

At the same time, more of the onus will shift on you to acquire more personal power. Your list of sources will be endless as your valuable knowledge base grows. Teacher stagnation and mediocrity will not be a part of your teaching world.

The saying, "You stop teaching when you stop learning" has a new and deeper meaning. The mindset of being "Ever ready to learn" becomes a teacher weapon that is easy, fun and powerful. Start immediately to compile your own notes to expand your references and begin your journey towards a real horizon.

TEACH DON'T PREACH

By constantly expanding your references, you are not limited to an in-service, seminar or educational program to help solve your teaching challenges. Instead, you are enriching your life, and applying your constantly growing repertoire of weapons to your teaching. This is how all of the teacher weapons that are covered in this book were developed.

In my 30 plus years in education, there were only two programs that I found to be superior and had lasting power, *The Morning Program and the TQM Integrated with Effective Schools Research.*

MORNING PROGRAM,
"WAKE UP EVERYBODY, THE DAY IS WASTING"

The Morning Program is the first of two exceptional school programs that have lasting power. Please be aware that many of the teacher weapons contained in this book can be found in this program. The Morning Program is a 20-minute daily assembly in school that includes all of the students, staff, teachers, principal and any visiting parents.

The purpose of this program is learning, and not merely entertainment. There is a close correlation of the Morning Program's goals and objectives as they relate to the learning standards of New York State and the school district.

This program places a positive start to each day for everyone. It promotes a positive resonance throughout the school. The Morning Program fosters a peaceful school, a powerful learning environment, and arranges for a daily school and parent connection.

There are many programs contained in this Morning Program, too numerous to mention; however, they are **all** geared to student learning. The hard work of the teachers and staff makes this one of the best programs that I ever participated in. This program is an excellent vehicle for real teaching and real learning.

TQM AND EFFECTIVE SCHOOLS

Soon after The Morning Program was in full swing, a second program was started. This excellent program also had lasting power. "TQM (Total Quality Management) Integrated with Effective Schools Research" proved to be a superior program. It enabled our school to reach very high levels in teaching and learning.

This was proven in the very first year when our students received excellent results on the New York State tests. The instructor of this program was Bill Rauhauser, Ph.D. He was very much like those special few martial arts instructors. He was not just any teacher or presenter of a program. His knowledge base was extensive and his pragmatic applications to our school were phenomenal.

He truly possessed a high level of vision and wisdom in the field of school improvement. His skill and dedication made it a privilege and an honor to work with him. Bill Rauhauser is a **real** teacher and not just a preacher. On many occasions, he rolled up his sleeves and guided us in the right direction to solve the many challenges that would surface. This program, along with its instructor, helped us not just to survive, but to thrive.

Both of these programs had a very positive and powerful effect on the school. They were voluntary programs that were not forced upon the teachers and staff. They helped in the achievement of very high standards: academically, attitudinally and behaviorally. The educational atmosphere that existed in this school became exemplary. These programs are still powerful and very effective even after years of their initial implementation.

The educational presenters of these programs showed how embraceable and exceptional the programs could be. An ongoing system of help was part of each program until the school's independence was achieved.

However, it was the hard work and dedication of everyone at the school that made these programs extraordinary. The faculty was the heart and soul of these programs. They were unrelenting energizer buddies. These teachers did not preach to anyone, but instead, worked smart and hard.

Their energy and enthusiasm was very focused into making these programs extraordinary. They demonstrated that exemplary teaching takes place with a little bit of talking, and a whole lot of action. Real learning takes place in much the same way. Preaching requires much talking, but exemplary teaching and learning requires action.

These two excellent programs armed the staff of this school with an arsenal of weapons to combat the many challenges that teachers face each day.

FOUR PHASES IN PURSUIT OF TEACHER EXCELLENCE

In an ongoing pursuit to be excellent teachers and educators, we matriculated through the different phases that provided continuous growth. They are:

1. Use facts and information to acquire knowledge
2. Repeatedly apply this knowledge in a practical way to prove its value
3. Describe this clearly and concisely as a teacher weapon
4. Use this process throughout your career to proceed on a path where few have reached

TEACHERS, BE ARMED AND POWERFUL

Every teacher has the potential to be a positive and powerful force that can have a lasting effect on students. However, this doesn't just happen because we want it to happen. The teachers that have this effect on their students are extraordinary. These teachers achieve a level higher than most of their colleagues, because they are in an unrelenting pursuit to continually grow.

This pursuit enables one to develop, discover, utilize and refine the teacher weapons in *Martial Arts of the Mind for Teachers*. These teacher weapons can enable you to be armed and powerful. Remember, these weapons **are** allowed in school. So don't hesitate to use them and reap the benefits.

Use this book as a springboard in your pursuit to continually grow as a teacher. So be a teacher who continues to be powerful. It's not always easy, but it certainly is attainable.

Just a Thought …

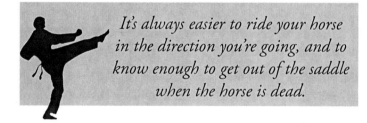

It's always easier to ride your horse in the direction you're going, and to know enough to get out of the saddle when the horse is dead.

Summary of Teacher Weapons

TEACHER WEAPON DESCRIPTION

1. Develop a powerful focus (Chap. 2)
2. Develop eyes in the back of your head (Chap. 2)
3. An honorable teaching attitude (Chap. 3 & 9)
4. Leadership application of an honorable attitude (Chap. 3)
5. The 90% solution (Chap. 3)
6. Leadership application of the 90% solution (Chap. 3)
7. Teacher daily preparedness (Chap. 4)
8. Managing your teacher accumulations (Chap. 4)
9. *Teacher randori* – prioritize (Chap. 5)
10. Taking immediate action (Chap. 5)
11. Mental preparation for test taking (*high-stakes testing*) (Chap. 5)
12. The transforming power in your words (Chap. 6)
13. Emphasize the positive aspects and downplay the negative ones (Chap. 6)
14. Transforming resistance into assistance during difficult conferences (Chap. 6)
15. Replace worry and anxiety with action and satisfaction *(high-stakes testing)* (Chap. 7)
16. Eight-step teaching paradigm (*high stakes testing*) (Chap. 7)
17. Keeping your balance and center by not over training or over teaching (Chap. 7)
18. Moderation with discretion for teachers (Chap. 7)
19. Escaping off the teacher's plateau (Chap. 8)
20. *Teacher ukemi* (Chap. 8)
21. There is no real answer key (Chap. 8)

Reference List

Armstrong, T., 1994. Multiple Intelligences in the Classroom. Alexandria: Association For Supervision and Curriculum Development.

Bennis, W., and B. Nanus, 1985. Leaders: Strategies for Taking Charge. New York: Harper & Row.

Biancolli, L., trans. 1966. The Divine Comedy/Paradise. New York: Washington Square Press.

Conner, E., 1987. Marie Curie. illus.by Richard Hook. New York: Book Wright Press.

Dobson, T., and V. Miller, 1993. Aikido in Everyday Life: Giving in to Get Your Way. Berekeley: North Atlantic Books.

Merriam-Webster's Collegiate Dictionary. 11th ed. Springfield, MA: Merriam-Webster, 2003. Also available online at http://www.Merriam-WebsterCollegiate.com and as a CD.-ROM.

Michie, J. trans.and sel.,2002. The Epigrams of Martial. New York: Modern Library.

O'Connor, G., 1993. The Aikido Student Handbook. Berkeley: Frog, Ltd.

Rauhauser, W., unpublished. The Quality Planning Book for Building Level School Improvement Teams.

Rauhauser, W., and A. McLennan, 1995. America's Schools Making Them Work. Chappel Hill: New View Publications.

Robbins, A., 1987. Unlimited Power. New York: Ballentine Books.

Robbins, A., 1991. Awaken The Giant Within. New York: Summit Books.

Reference List
(Continued)

Saotome, M., 1993. Aikido and the Harmony of Nature. Boston: Shambhala Publications, Inc.

Saotome, M., and H. Ikeda, Third Edition. ASU Training Handbook. Self-Published.

Sawyer, R., trans. 1996. The Complete Art Of War / Sun Tzu / Sun Pin. Boulder: Westview Press.

Soothill, W., trans. 1995. The Analects / Confucius. New York: Dover Publications, Inc.

Stevens, J., trans., comp. 1992. The Art of Peace Teachings of the Founder of Aikido. Boston: Shambhala Publications, Inc.

Breinigsville, PA USA
14 June 2010
239873BV00004B/14/P